CUSTOMER SERVICE GAMES
FOR TRAINING

Customer Service Games for Training

GRAHAM ROBERTS-PHELPS

Gower

Published by
Gower Publishing Limited
Gower House
Croft Road
Aldershot
Hampshire GU11 3HR
England

Gower
131 Main Street
Burlington
Vermont 05401
USA

British Library Cataloguing in Publication Data

Roberts-Phelps, Graham
    Customer service games for training
    1. Customer services – Employees – Training of 2. Management
    games
    I. Title
    658.8'12

    ISBN 0 566 08205 5

Library of Congress Cataloging-in-Publication Data

Roberts-Phelps, Graham.
    Customer service games for training / Graham Roberts-Phelps.
        p.   cm.
    ISBN 0-566-08205-5 (hardback)
    1. Customer services. 2. Employees – Training of – Problems, exercises, etc. 3. Management games. I. Title.

HF5415.5 .R625 2000
658.8'12–dc21   00-042960

Typeset in 11 point Palatino by Bournemouth Colour Press, Parkstone and printed in Great Britain by MPG Books Limited, Bodmin.

Contents

Introduction

About this book

The games and activities in this have been created for the training of service skills. Relevant to all types of industry and successful with personnel of any age, experience and background, they are designed with the following characteristics in mind.

Easy to run

Simple to follow, step-by-step instructions mean that a minimum of preparation and experience is required. The time saved can be devoted to either enhancing the basic activity or creating company-specific material.

Complete

Each activity comes with everything necessary – handouts, worksheets and OHP slides.

Generic

Whether you are a manufacturer or a service provider, private or public sector, industrial or retail, the games and activities are focused on generic customer service knowledge and skills – skills that are completely transferable across all organizations and situations. Most use an 'open content' approach, which means that participants use their own examples and experiences as the main subject, making the exercises automatically and completely relevant. (They are, of course, easy to customize should you wish to do so.)

Varied

The activities range from 15-minute ice-breakers to 90-minute role plays and include games, questionnaires, problem-solving activities and discussions. This means that the training can be kept varied and interesting, and topics approached from several different angles.

Open in content

As the 'content' of many of the games and activities is provided by the participants themselves, the material is instantly relevant and appropriate.

How to use this book

Each activity is detailed in a clear set of instructions for the trainer, with information contained under the following headings.

Summary

This gives a brief outline of the activity.

Purpose

It is a good idea to share the objectives with the participants in order to help them focus on the activity's purpose.

Format

This gives the recommended grouping of participants to best carry out the activity.

Type

This gives the category which the activity falls under – for example, ice-breaker or skill-builder.

Suitable for

This shows what type or level of customer service personnel will most benefit from the activity.

Resources

This is a brief checklist of what is needed to run the activity.

Time

Here, the estimated time needed to run the activity, based on a group size of between eight and ten participants, is indicated. The time required may be shorter or longer if the group is smaller or larger than this. The estimates err on the side of generosity, as activities tend to overrun rather than underrun. Any extra time allowed also gives trainers an opportunity to expand the activity with their own material or examples.

Procedure

This section details the training instructions and explains how to introduce, run and conclude each activity. These instructions are kept deliberately brief so that the information you need can be easily found, read and relayed to the group while you are running the activity.

Instructions have been phrased in a general way and, where possible, avoid suggesting the actual words to be used, as very few trainers will use them, preferring instead to communicate in their own personal style.

Discussion points

This is a list, provided in some activities, of useful points for developing and expanding a discussion during the activity. Each point is accompanied by a space for you to add your own thoughts and ideas, either when preparing for the activity or as a result of running it.

Handouts

Handouts, denoted by a 🖹 symbol, usually contain instructions to participants on how to perform a task or activity, or may be in the form of a worksheet. Written handouts provide participants with a reference during the exercise making communication much clearer.

The main formats of the games and activities

Individuals

When participants are required to work on their own, perhaps completing a questionnaire or worksheet, it allows for a degree of self-reflection and makes an excellent contrast to the role play and group work. Many people are happy working in this way; indeed, it follows the pattern of learning established at school.

Pairs

Based on the principle that 'two heads are better than one', this format needs participants to work in pairs, working through a problem, questionnaire or worksheet jointly.

It is useful to pair people carefully, balancing personalities and experience. Make sure that both are contributing and making notes. On longer courses it is a good idea to change these pairs occasionally. If you have an odd number of participants, one group can be stretched to three.

Small groups

Small groups of 3–8 people are most suitable for working on a problem, issue or discussion as well as for free-format ideas sessions.

The size of your main group will, of course, determine how many small groups you can have, but, generally, it is difficult to circulate between, or monitor, more than about four groups.

Main group discussion

This is a format in which you may run a general discussion or activity with the whole group of eight or more people.

You may like to experiment and develop your own variations of the games and activities as you run them. You will also find that, because of the 'open-content' nature of the activities, they will vary slightly in execution, with different groups having different reactions and results.

Role plays

The series of role plays included in the book can be used in isolation or as ongoing exercises during a training course. The role-play customers can be based on real customers taken from existing accounts. Alternatively, you may wish to create your own sample case studies.

Five tips to get the best out of this book

1. *Use the exercises with confidence*

> All the activities and games in this book have been developed and used in professional training courses and seminars, and are all proven to be effective on different types of course and with a variety of participants.

2. *Be flexible*

> Because of their 'open content' style, the activities are suitable for most types of organization and training course. This approach also makes them easy to adapt to fit your needs. You might want to experiment and develop your own variations of these games and activities – for example, by adding in new elements or extending various segments. You will also find that no two activities are ever the same, as each group of participants will shape each one slightly differently.

3. *Structure your training*

> By mixing at least three different formats (working in small groups or pairs, as individuals and in the group as a whole) to cover the same points, you can greatly increase learning retention and effectiveness. People will differ in their working preferences, and everyone will gain more if the formats are varied throughout the course.

4. *Make notes and adapt*

> Don't be afraid to customize or edit these activities to suit your own training style as you gain experience in running them. Make notes in the margins, either while preparing or during a course to remind you of the points next time.

5. *Train, don't talk*

> Much of the trainer's time is spent not telling people what to do, but trying to get them to **do** what they already **know**. These activities and games are designed to help people learn. If you find yourself talking rather less than you might do normally, don't worry about it!

Part I

The Games and Activities

1   Artists in action

Summary   Working in pairs, participants are asked to reproduce a picture by following a verbally communicated description.

Purpose   To highlight the importance of clarity in both explaining and listening. Also to demonstrate how we can 'impose' our interpretation of what is said.

Format   Pairs.

Type   Energizer

Suitable for   All customer service staff.

Resources   A simple picture or photograph for each pair.
A sheet of paper and a pencil for each pair.

Time   10–15 minutes.

Procedure
1. Ask the participants to work with a partner. One is an artist. The other is the artist's assistant. They are each other's customer. The goal of the exercise for the artist is to use listening skills and customer-focused attitudes in order to produce the picture that the assistant describes.
2. Ask the pairs to decide which partner is the assistant and which the artist. They should sit back-to-back
3. Pass a simple picture, taken from a book or magazine, or a photograph to the assistant in each pair. He or she should not show the picture to the artist.
4. The assistant should now describe their picture to the artist who will attempt to reproduce it from the description. The artist should listen as the assistant describes the picture and then use questions and restate their understanding to explore the directions they have received.
5. Allow eight minutes to complete the activity.

6. Finally, ask each of the pairs for feedback on how they felt about the activity and what they found easy or difficult.

2   Bars of soap

Summary   A pair of volunteers read out a written exchange of notes between a hotel customer and a maid.

Purpose   To highlight how, even with the best intentions, we can still frustrate our customers!

Format   Main group.

Type   Ice-breaker/Energizer

Suitable for   All levels of customer service staff.

Resources   Two copies of the handout.

Time   10 minutes or as required.

Procedure

1. Ask for two volunteers. Invite them to the front of the room and give each a copy of the handout. Allocate one volunteer to read the customer role and the other to read the maid/hotel responses. The hotel/maid responses are in italics.
2. Ask the rest of participants to listen and enjoy!

11

Bars of soap

Here is some correspondence which actually occurred between a staff member of a London hotel and one of its guests. The London hotel involved submitted this to a national newspaper. No name was mentioned.

Dear Maid, Please do not leave any more of those little bars of soap in my bathroom since I have brought my own bath-sized Dial. Please remove the six unopened little bars from the shelf under the medicine chest and another three in the shower soap dish. They are in my way. Thank you, S. Berman.

Dear Room 635, I am not your regular maid. She will be back tomorrow, Thursday, from her day off. I took the 3 hotel soaps out of the shower soap dish as you requested. The 6 bars on your shelf I took out of your way and put on top of your Kleenex dispenser in case you should change your mind. This leaves only the 3 bars I left today, as my instructions from the management is to leave 3 soaps daily. I hope this is satisfactory. Kathy, Relief Maid.

Dear Maid, I hope you are my regular maid. Apparently Kathy did not tell you about my note to her concerning the little bars of soap. When I got back to my room this evening I found you had added 3 little Camays to the shelf under my medicine cabinet. I am going to be here in the hotel for two weeks and have brought my own bath-sized Dial so I won't need those 6 little Camays which are on the shelf. They are in my way when shaving, brushing teeth, etc. Please remove them. S. Berman.

Dear Mr Berman, My day off was last Wednesday so the relief maid left 3 hotel soaps as we are instructed to do by the management. I took the 6 soaps which were in your way on the shelf and put them in the soap dish where your Dial was. I put the Dial in the medicine cabinet for your convenience. I didn't remove the 3 complimentary soaps which are always placed inside the medicine cabinet for all new check-ins and which you did not object to when you checked in last Monday. Please let me know if I can be of further assistance. Your regular maid, Dotty.

cont'd

Reproduced from *Customer Service Games for Training*, Graham Roberts-Phelps, Gower, Aldershot

Dear Mr Berman, The assistant manager, Mr Kensedder, informed me this am that you called him last evening and said you were unhappy with your maid service. I have assigned a new girl to your room. I hope you will accept my apologies for any past inconvenience. If you have any future complaints please contact me so I can give it my personal attention. Call extension 1108 between 8am and 5pm. Thank you. Elaine Carmen, Housekeeper.

Dear Miss Carmen, It is impossible to contact you by phone since I leave the hotel for business at 7.45 am and don't get back before 5.30 or 6 pm. That's the reason I called Mr Kensedder last night. You were already off duty. I only asked Mr Kensedder if he could do anything about those little bars of soap. The new maid you assigned me must have thought I was a new check-in today, since she left another 3 bars of hotel soap in my medicine cabinet along with her regular delivery of 3 bars on the bathroom shelf. In just 5 days here I have accumulated 24 little bars of soap. Why are you doing this to me? S. Berman.

Dear Mr Berman, Your maid, Kathy, has been instructed to stop delivering soap to your room and remove the extra soaps. If I can be of further assistance, please call extension 1108 between 8 am and 5 pm. Thank you, Elaine Carmen, Housekeeper.

Dear Mr Kensedder, My bath size Dial is missing. Every bar of soap was taken from my room including my own bath size Dial. I came in late last night and had to call the bellhop to bring me 4 little Cashmere Bouquets. S. Berman.

Dear Mr Berman, I have informed our housekeeper, Elaine Carmen, of your soap problem. I cannot understand why there was no soap in your room since our maids are instructed to leave 3 bars of soap each time they service a room. The situation will be rectified immediately. Please accept my apologies for the inconvenience. Martin L. Kensedder, Assistant Manager.

Dear Mrs Carmen, Who the hell left 54 little bars of Camay in my room? I came in last night and found 54 little bars of soap. I don't want 54 little bars of Camay. I want my one damn bar of bath-sized Dial. Do you realize I have 54 bars of soap in here? All I want is my bath-sized Dial. Please give me back my bath-sized Dial. S. Berman.

cont'd

Reproduced from *Customer Service Games for Training*, Graham Roberts-Phelps, Gower, Aldershot

Dear Mr Berman, You complained of too much soap in your room so I had them removed. Then you complained to Mr Kensedder that all your soap was missing so I personally returned them. The 24 Camays which had been taken and the 3 Camays you are supposed to receive daily [sic]. I don't know anything about the 4 Cashmere Bouquets. Obviously your maid, Kathy, did not know I had returned your soaps so she also brought 24 Camays plus the 3 daily Camays. I don't know where you got the idea this hotel issues bath-sized Dial. I was able to locate some bath-sized Ivory which I left in your room. Elaine Carmen, Housekeeper.

Dear Mrs. Carmen, Just a short note to bring you up to date on my latest soap inventory. As of today I possess:

- on shelf under medicine cabinet 18 Camay in 4 stacks of 4 and 1 stack of 2
- on Kleenex dispenser 11 Camay in 2 stacks of 4 and 1 stack of 3
- on bedroom dresser 1 stack of 3 Cashmere Bouquet, 1 stack of 4 hotel size Ivory, and 8 Camay in 2 stacks of 4
- inside medicine cabinet 14 Camay in 3 stacks of 4 and 1 stack of 2
- in shower soap dish 6 Camay, very moist
- on north-east corner of tub 1 Cashmere Bouquet, slightly used
- on north-west corner of tub 6 Camays in 2 stacks of 3.

Please ask Kathy when she services my room to make sure the stacks are neatly piled and dusted. Also, please advise her that stacks of more than 4 have a tendency to tip. May I suggest that my bedroom windowsill is not in use and will make an excellent spot for future soap deliveries. One more item, I have purchased another bar of bath-sized Dial which I am keeping in the hotel vault in order to avoid further misunderstandings. S. Berman.

3 Communication dynamics

Summary
Participants work in small groups to discuss and agree a consensus on the relative significance of words, voice tone and body language in face-to-face communication.

Purpose
To introduce the themes of body language and voice tone in customer service.

Format
Main or small groups.

Type
Subject breaker.

Suitable for
Customer service staff who deal with customers face-to-face.

Resources
A handout for each participant.

Time
20 minutes.

Procedure
1. Introduce the activity by explaining that it is commonly accepted that human communication falls into three categories – words, voice tone and body language.
2. Distribute the handout and ask the participants to work individually and decide which of these three elements is the most significant in dealing with customers face-to-face. Allow 3 minutes.
3. Next, divide the participants into groups of 2–3.
4. Allow 5–10 minutes for the small groups to compare their pie charts and arrive at a group consensus.
5. Reconvene the main group and collect their ratings. Discuss the issues and examples that reinforce the significance of voice tone and body language.

The generally agreed split is: words = 7%; voice tone = 38%; body language = 55%.

Discussion points

- How do you judge people's moods and emotions?

- How do you know when someone is lying or misleading you?

- Do you ever 'know' what someone is thinking?

- How many different ways can you say 'I did not steal the chocolate' to create a subtle different meaning each time? (Try saying the sentence and emphasize the words 'I', 'steal' and 'chocolate' differently each time.)

Communication dynamics

Using the empty circle below, draw a pie chart to show the percentage that each of the following make up in our face-to-face communication:

- Words   _____ %

- Voice tone   _____ %

- Body language   _____ %

                                100%

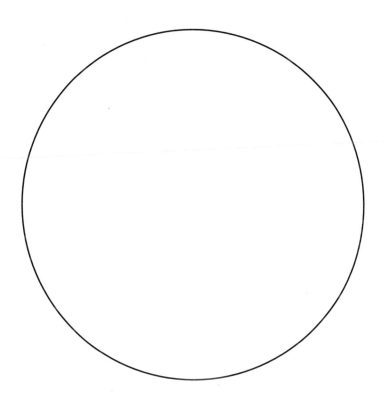

4 Complaints as opportunities

Summary   Participants work individually and then in small groups to recall their own experiences of service problems and how they were handled.

Purpose   To illustrate the value of 'service recovery'. A well handled complaint will often *increase* a customer's loyalty.

Format   Individuals and small groups.

Type   Subject breaker.

Suitable for   All customer service staff.

Resources   A copy of the handout for each participant.
A flipchart and pens.

Time   20–30 minutes.

Procedure   1. Start by explaining that research has shown that when a customer's problem is handled well, the customer will be more loyal, and perhaps more 'satisfied', than they would had there been no problem at all.
2. Distribute a copy of the handout to each participant and ask them to individually make notes on the questions. Allow 10 minutes.
3. Form participants into groups of 2–3.
4. Allow 5–10 minutes for the group members to compare their notes. The purpose is, through discussion, to arrive at a summary of the following key points within their group.

● How did each group member feel about poor service?

- How did they feel about the organization's response to their problem?
- What conclusions can they draw about the effect of good complaint handling on customers' attitudes.

5. Reconvene all the participants and ask each group in turn to review their findings. Summarize their ideas and notes on a flipchart.

Discussion points

- How would you develop a 'policy' towards handling complaints?

- What are the most important things to do first?

- What annoys customers most – faulty products, poor procedures or rude/unhelpful people?

- How could we take these ideas and relate them to our role of providing customer service and satisfaction?

Complaints as opportunities

1. Think of a recent negative service experience you've had as a customer. Describe it briefly below.

2. What three words describe how you *felt* at the time?

3. What did the organization do in response to the problem?

4. How did you feel about its response?

5. What would you have liked it to do?

5   Customer confessions

Summary	Participants share experiences and reflect on the different types of customer they encounter – good, bad and amusing!
Purpose	To explore different perceptions of customers.
Format	Individuals.
Type	Ice-breaker/energizer.
Suitable for	All levels of customer service staff.
Resources	A handout for each participant.
Time	20–30 minutes.
Procedure	1. Introduce the activity by stating its purpose as set out above. 2. Distribute a copy of the handout to each participant. Ask them to work individually for 5 minutes, writing answers in the space for each customer. 3. Ask each participant in turn to read out their answers.
Variation	Ask the participants to write their answers on a flipchart page or OHP slide and either pin the page on the wall or present to the whole group.

Customer confessions

> **My favourite type of customer is:**

> **My worst type of customer is:**

> **My best ever customer experience was:**

> **My worst ever customer experience was:**

> **My most amusing customer experience was:**

6 Customer feedback: performance versus expectation

Summary   Participants work in small groups to rate aspects of customer service, in terms of their importance to customers, and how well they are performed. The variation between expectation and performance provides a starting point for action.

Purpose   To understand and gain a method for analysing results from customer survey forms or satisfaction research. Participants may also apply their own views as to the performance of key elements – in terms of both the relative importance to the customer and current performance – and, in this way, identify areas of over- and underperformance.

Format   Small groups.

Type   Improving methods.

Suitable for All levels of customer service staff, including managers and supervisors.

Resources   Copies of the two handouts for each participant.
Flipchart and marker pens.
Survey data (optional).

Time   45–60 minutes.

Procedure   This activity can be carried out using real data from customer surveys or can be based on participants' working knowledge and familiarity with customer responses.

1. Introduce the activity by stating the purpose set out above.
2. With the group, review examples of the ten or so elements on which the analysis will be based. These might be taken from the survey forms that you will be analysing or be suggested by yourself or the group. Distribute copies of the two handouts – 'Performance vs expectation' and 'Customer feedback analysis' to each participant.
3. Next divide the participants into small groups, and ask them to complete the exercise. Encourage them to discuss each element fully, before making their ratings. Allow 25–30 minutes.
   - Ask each group to transfer their conclusions to a flipchart and present back to the whole group.

Variation   Use the ratings to develop an action plan. Start by addressing elements where performance is not meeting expectation. You may also choose to add in another element at this stage and rate each of the elements according to the ease or difficulty involved in improving them. The action plan should focus on those areas of most significant underperformance that are also the easiest to improve.

Customer feedback: performance vs expectation

1. Identify ten elements of customer service, trying to cover all aspects of your job. These might include speed, accuracy, helpfulness, follow-up – you can choose your own criteria. List them in the box below.

2. Rate each of these ten elements according to the importance that customers attach to it, 1 being important and 10 being critically important. You can use any customer feedback you have gathered to help you with your rating. Alternatively, just put yourself in your customer's shoes and prepare the rating according to your experience. Enter the figures in column A.

3. Now rate the same service elements according to how well you deliver them, 1 being very poorly and 10 representing excellently. Enter the figures in column B.

4. Subtract the figure A from figure B. Remove the + or – sign from the result and list it in the 'Variance' column. In other words, if A=10 (very high) and B=4 (low), or alternatively A=2 (low) and B=8 (high), the answer in both cases is 6.

5. You now have a measure for how your delivery of each of these service elements differs from your customer's expectation. If you wish, you can use the customer feedback analysis handout to illustrate your findings.

   If you are underperforming, you'll need to address this. Equally in some measures, an overperformance may reflect too much time (and possibly money) spent on the element. Alternatively, this might be an aspect that you could promote to customers, so that it begins to feature more prominently in their expectations.

Element of service/performance or perception	Importance to customer (A)	Performance rating (B)	Variance; c (=B–A)
1			
2			
3			

cont'd

Element of service/performance or perception	Importance to customer (A)	Performance rating (B)	Variance; c (=B–A)
4			
5			
6			
7			
8			
9			
10			

Reproduced from *Customer Service Games for Training*, Graham Roberts-Phelps, Gower, Aldershot

Performance vs expectation: customer feedback analysis

Transfer each of the elements listed in the previous part of the exercise and plot on the graph where the two points intersect. For example, if you had 'welcoming smile' as an element with a score of 8 for importance and a score of 7 for performance, this would be placed towards the centre of Quadrant B.

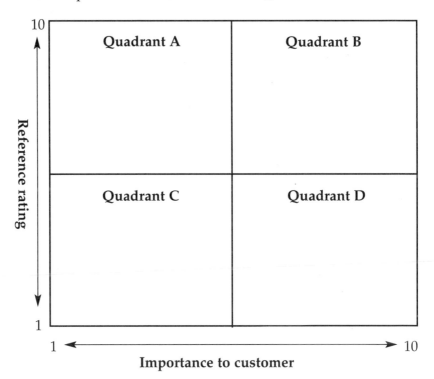

Notes

Quadrant A: You may be overdelivering these aspects of service. If this implies a cost to your organization, look at ways of reducing it. Alternatively, how might you increase the importance of this aspect of service in your customers' eyes?

Quadrant B: Aspects of your service that fall into this quadrant represent issues that are important to your customers and on which you perform well. Use these to help distinguish your service from that of your competitors.

cont'd

Reproduced from *Customer Service Games for Training*, Graham Roberts-Phelps, Gower, Aldershot

Quadrant C: This quadrant represents service aspects that are insignificant to customers and to which you give little priority. Remember that all customers are different – don't miss those few customers for whom these aspects may be important.

Quadrant D: This quadrant represents the most immediate areas for attention. It shows service aspects that are important to your customers but which you may be underdelivering.

7 Customer service call flow diagram

Summary   Participants are introduced to a model for the structure and skills needed for a successful telephone call and are asked to work in small groups to construct a flow diagram of telephone customer service in their organization.

Purpose   To help participants focus and reflect on each of the constituent parts in the service that they deliver.

Format   Small groups.

Type   Analysis of process and procedures.

Suitable for   All customer service staff.

Resources   Copies of the two handouts for each participant.
Paper and pens for each small group.

Time   30–40 minutes.

Procedure
1. Explain the purpose of the activity as described above.
2. State that good service standards must be consistent to be truly effective: charm and friendliness are important, but so is achieving things quickly and efficiently.
3. Explain that this activity asks them to consider the sequence, process, order and system that they use to serve customers, and consequently how they might improve things. As an example, ask if anybody knows why we use a QWERTY keyboard layout. The answer is that this layout is designed to slow down the typist's speed as in the early days of typewriters they kept jamming and breaking if they typed too quickly. The problem no longer exists, but we still use the same system!

4. Distribute a copy of the two handouts, 'Customer Service Call Flow Diagram' and 'Telephone Call Structure' to each participant. Explain that the Telephone Call Structure illustrates the process and skills of handling an internal call and that the Call Flow Diagram shows how these have been applied to an example from a company supplying computers.

5. Allow everyone 2–3 minutes to study both diagrams and then invite questions.

6. Divide the participants into smaller groups of 3–6 and ask each of them to use the Telephone Call Structure to prepare a flow diagram of their own telephone call structure. Make sure that everyone is clear on the task and then allow 20–25 minutes to complete the exercise.

7. Once the allotted time has passed, ask each group to post their flowcharts round the room for the others to look at after the session.

8. Invite the groups to share any conclusions they have reached about the process they use for telephone customer service.

Variations and options

- This activity can be adapted and used for most functional tasks – for example, credit control, order fulfilment, administration and so on.
- This activity can also provide a starting point for an action planning session to improve aspects of the way in which telephone customer service is delivered.

Customer service call flow diagram: example

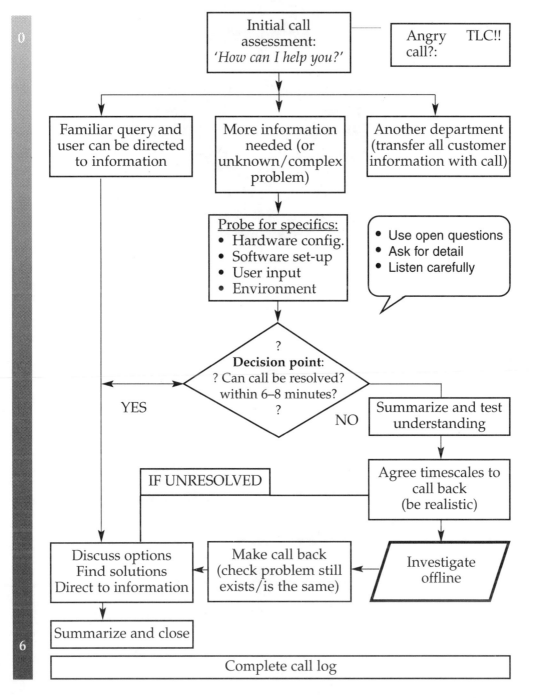

Telephone call structure

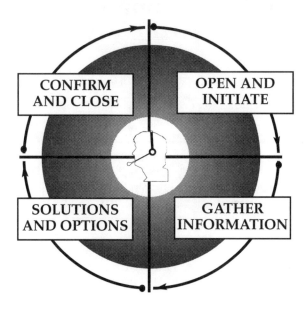

Key Skills

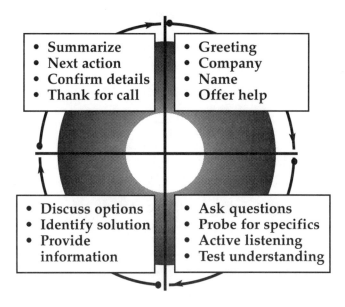

8 Customer service buzz groups

Summary   Small groups of participants brainstorm suggested customer service discussion issues and present back to the whole group.

Purpose   To focus on some of the fundamental issues behind the service you give to your customers and help service staff reflect on these issues for themselves.

Format   Small groups.

Type   Ice-breaker/energizer.

Suitable for   All levels of customer service staff.

Resources   A flipchart and marker pens.

Time   20–30 minutes.

Procedure
1. Introduce the activity by stating the purpose set out above.
2. Divide the participants into groups of four or more people, perhaps scattered around the room or in separate rooms.
3. Give each group the same topic **or** a different topic to discuss (see 'Discussion topics' below). Ask one member of each group to act as a facilitator, encouraging and guiding discussion and making notes on a notepad or flipchart page. Allow 15–20 minutes.
4. Ask each group to present back in turn to the whole group when the time is up.

Discussion topics
1. What is our mission statement? (The mission statement should be a summary of all the following points as well.) *Use*

only if there is no written mission statement in existence for the organization or department.

2. What product do we produce? What are the components of the integrated products/services, distribution network, support services, departmental relationships and so forth?
3. Who are our customers? What are the principal subgroupings of customers or market segments?
4. Where are our customers? Geographically? In terms of level in their organization? How many steps are there between us and them? How do they get our products?
5. What do our customers buy? How close is it to what they need? How do we know?
6. What is our relationship with our customers? How do we know they are getting what they need? How do they learn how to use our products?
7. What do they do with what they buy?
8. Who are our known competitors? Who else provides products or services that could be substituted for ours in the customer's eyes? Who will our competitors be tomorrow?
9. What is it that our customers most value about our organization (not just our products)? About our competitors?
10. What trends in our customers' businesses or lifestyles are likely to change what they will need from us?

Variation   Write one topic on a flipchart page or OHP slide and facilitate a discussion with the whole group.

9 Customer service examples

Summary

Working in small groups, participants recall and share examples of good and bad service that they have experienced as customers.

Purpose

To appreciate service from the customer's point of view, and to identify the experience, knowledge and attitude prevalent in the group.

Format

Small groups.

Type

Ice-breaker/energizer.

Suitable for

All levels of customer service staff.

Resources

A copy of the handout for each participant.
A flipchart and marker pens.

Time

40–50 minutes.

Procedure

1. Divide the participants into small groups of 3–6.
2. Distribute a copy of the handout to each participant.
3. Ask the participants to work, in their groups, as directed on the handout. Encourage everyone to relate their stories as fully as possible – what happened, who said/did what and so forth. Allow 15–20 minutes for this.
4. Monitor the groups as required, keeping track of time.
5. Reconvene the whole group and ask each group to present their findings in turn, using a flipchart.
6. Discuss the presentations with the group as a whole.

Discussion points

- How many of the examples of good service represent

'service recovery' – that is, winning back a customer by handling a complaint or problem effectively?

- What are the principal causes of customer dissatisfaction? Are they small things or bad attitudes rather than major problems?

- How many of the bad examples involve the attitude of the customer service staff?

- What are the similarities between examples?

Customer service examples

1. Working in your group discuss examples of good and bad customer service that you have experienced **as a customer**. List at least three of each.
2. Be sure to examine each case in detail, identifying what impressed or depressed you in each case.
3. Select one member of your group to present back your findings to the whole group, when asked.

Good examples	Bad examples

Reproduced from *Customer Service Games for Training*, Graham Roberts-Phelps, Gower, Aldershot

10 Customer skills 1: being prepared

Summary   Participants work in pairs on a case study and list ways in which the subject of the study could have been better prepared for the situation.

Purpose   To consider the importance of preparation – in particular how being prepared can help create a good first impression.

Format   Individuals and pairs.

Type   Skill-builder.

Suitable for   All levels of customer service staff.

Resources   A handout for each participant.
A flipchart and marker pens.

Time   20–25 minutes.

Procedure   1. Introduce the activity by stating the purpose set out above.
2. Distribute a copy of the handout to each participant and ask them to read it individually.
3. Now have the participants work in pairs to make a list of ideas as to what the subject of the story could have done to have been more prepared. Allow 10 minutes.
4. After 10 minutes have passed, review the key points from the group as a whole, listing them on a flipchart.

Variation   Create alternatives based on your (or the participants') work and customer profile.

Discussion points
- Of the three kinds of customer needs associated with being

prepared to serve customers, which one are you best prepared to meet on a daily basis? Why?
- Informational
- Physical
- Emotional

Why?

● Which of the three customer needs do you most need to improve your ability to meet in order to serve your customers? Why?

Customer skills 1: being prepared

Please read the following:

Being prepared is the first stage of the customer relationship process. As a customer, you often know within the first few minutes of a visit or call to a company or co-worker whether you are glad you made the visit or call and whether you will be provided with good service. These first impressions frequently depend on how you are received.

As a provider, you want to welcome customers and let them know you appreciate their business and their input. To focus on the customer in the receiving stage means treating each customer as a valued individual. How the customer is received may determine whether he or she continues to want to do business with you and your organization.

What does it take to make a good job of receiving customers? Two skills are required:

- Be ready.
- Welcome the customer.

Case study: Part 1 – being prepared

It is a rather quiet Monday morning. Everything in your work area seems to be in order. You have been at your job for some time now, and you generally know what to expect. You know the questions that customers will ask before they even open their mouths, and you usually know the answers.

Today you feel quite ready to handle any tough problem or challenging customer who might come along. 'Emotionally prepared' is how you describe yourself. As you scan your work area, you say to yourself, 'This is too good to be true. Any minute now it'll get busy. But I'm ready.'

Pouring yourself a cup of coffee, you settle into your chair and begin to look through the mail in your in-box, and then…

Case study: Part 2 – priming

Within minutes, your calm, quiet morning erupts into a blaze of activity.

cont'd

The telephone rings. It is a co-worker wanting to transfer a call from a customer who has been having problems with his invoicing. Because you are able to answer virtually any billing question, you accept the call only to discover that the customer's account is handled by another office, not your own. Consequently, you cannot answer the customer's question, and he is irate at having been transferred twice already.

While you are still on the telephone with this customer, another co-worker rushes in to pick up a report which he left in your in-tray last week. You glanced at it briefly on Friday and noted that it required your review and input, but, since it was not due back until today, you put it aside. Your co-worker now tells you that your manager needs the report back for a presentation this afternoon. Rolling your eyes as the customer on the telephone continues to complain, you point your co-worker to a chair and begin to shuffle through your in-tray in search of the report.

Seconds later, the other telephone starts to ring. No one else in your area is picking up the call, so you put the irate customer on hold and pick up the new call yourself. It is a regular customer wanting to verify some status information quickly. Turning to your computer screen to access her information, you are faced by a message informing you that the network has been down for the past 15 minutes.

As you apologize to the second customer and explain that you are unable to access the information she needs, you notice that the other, irate customer has hung up and that your co-worker is halfway down the hall on his way to your manager's office with the unreviewed report in his hand…

Task

What could the person in this story have done to have been more prepared? Make a list.

Reproduced from *Customer Service Games for Training*, Graham Roberts-Phelps, Gower, Aldershot

11   Customer skills 2: welcoming

Summary   In this activity the trainer demonstrates, with a volunteer, three short role plays illustrating good, bad and indifferent welcoming skills. The participants then practise the skills for themselves.

Purpose   To identify the relevance of verbal and non-verbal cues in welcoming customers.

Format   Pairs or small groups.

Type   Skill-builder.

Suitable for   All levels of customer service staff.

Resources   Copies of the two handouts for each participant.
A flipchart and marker pens.

Time   20–30 minutes.

Procedure   1.   Introduce the activity by stating the purpose set out above.
2.   Distribute a copy of the handout, 'Welcoming', to each participant and ask them to read it individually.
3.   Ask for a volunteer to role-play three customer meetings. You will play the service provider and the volunteer will play the customer.
4.   Ask the group to watch and listen carefully to the three demonstration role plays that you are going to perform. Distribute the handout, 'Welcoming: worksheet', for making notes.
5.   Demonstrate three role plays of the first 1–2 minutes of a typical customer meeting or encounter. Play the first one for laughs, being deliberately rude or offhand. The second

should fairly neutral – not that bad – and the third should demonstrate how it should be done.

5. Lead a discussion on the different approaches and their effects on the customer transaction.

6. Finally, ask the participants to work in pairs or small groups to practise welcoming a customer themselves, using their own improvisations.

Variation   Video-record the role plays.

Discussion point   What can you do differently or better to improve the way in which you welcome your customers?

Welcoming

Welcoming a customer takes approximately 30 seconds. To deliver a truly effective welcoming statement, however, each of the following must consistently convey that you are ready and willing to focus on the customer.

- **Tone of voice**. The tone of voice that we use with customers often conveys more than we might expect. It is like a radio transmitting subtle sound waves or signals which tell them how we really feel about what we are doing. In other words, our attitude is conveyed through our voice. Aspects of voice tone include:
  - volume: soft or loud
  - fluctuation: varied or monotonous
  - clarity: clear or muffled
  - rate of speech: rapid or slow
  - emotion: hostile or pleasant.
- **Verbal language**. Language is verbal expression. It is what we use to introduce ourselves and to greet customers. In the brief welcoming phase, customers form opinions of us, in part from the words we use. Aspects of verbal language include:
  - attitude: courteous or uninterested
  - effectiveness: clear or jargon-laden
  - appropriateness: to the point or longwinded.
- **Body language**. Body language includes posture, gestures and facial expressions; like tone of voice, it communicates attitude. Physical behaviours signal to customers how we really feel about them and about what we are doing. Body language can be communicated over the telephone or in person; it has been proven that customers can actually receive a smile over the telephone. Aspects of body language include:
  - presence: energetic or apathetic
  - eye contact: direct or evasive
  - spatial proximity: close or distant
  - facial expression: smiling or expressionless.

Welcoming: worksheet

Role play example 1

    1.   What *tone of voice* did the provider use?

    2.   What did the provider's *verbal language* convey?

Role play example 2

    1.   What *tone of voice* did the provider use?

    2.   What did the provider's *verbal language* convey?

Role play example 3

    1.   What *tone of voice* did the provider use?

    2.   What did the provider's *verbal language* convey?

    3.   What did the provider's *body language* convey?

12   Customer skills 3: connecting

Summary   Participants work in pairs to learn about the skill of 'connecting' with customers – using listening and questioning skills to generate rapport and understanding.

Purpose   To formulate a set of 'high-gain' questions that can be used in a variety of situations to encourage customers to evaluate, analyse, speculate or express feelings.

Format   Pairs.

Type   Skill-builder.

Suitable for   All levels of customer service staff.

Resources   Copies of the three handouts for each participant.
A flipchart and marker pens.

Time   20–30 minutes.

Procedure
1. Introduce the activity by stating the purpose set out above.
2. Distribute the copies of the three handouts – 'Understanding', 'Asking effective questions' and 'Worksheet' – to each participant and ask them to read them through.
3. Next, ask the participants to work in pairs and use the worksheet to prepare a list of 'high-gain' questions that they might use with customers. You might wish to share some examples of your own first. Allow 10–15 minutes.
4. Reconvene the whole group and ask the pairs to shout out their questions. List them all on a flipchart and discuss.

Discussion points
- How do you connect quickly?
- How do you 'clear your mind' when approaching a customer or taking a call?
- What questions or topics work well?

Connecting: understanding

Connecting or understanding is the one of the most important and often the most difficult stage in serving customers because it requires you to concentrate completely on what the customer is saying. It can be particularly hard to remain focused on your customers when they call or stop by your office with the same questions and requests day after day. Yet, customers highly value the personalized attention you can give. A provider who focuses on the customer at this stage concentrates on everything the customer is saying – not only the words themselves, but also the way in which they are spoken – and responds in a manner that shows appreciation of, and concern for, the customer's feelings and needs.

The emphasis, during this stage, is on precisely identifying your customers' needs and expectations. In routine situations you may find that this requires only a brief conversation. At other times (for example, when your customer is unsure about what he or she needs or when the situation is complex), you may need to take more time to ensure that you understand clearly. In either situation, you must concentrate on the customer as an individual.

The skills you use to understand your customers are:

1. Listening for feelings and facts
2. Asking questions to clarify
3. Restating feelings and facts.

Listening to the feelings and facts, as stated by customers, is critical to maintaining a positive interaction and building trust and confidence with them. It is a skill that requires a great deal of concentration, especially in situations in which the customer is difficult or upset.

Connecting skills

How far you use skills 2 and 3 – asking and restating – depends on the complexity of the customer's requests and whether he or she is difficult or upset. For example, if you are performing a routine task for a customer, you will probably ask only a limited number of questions. The conversation is usually brief. However, if you are trying to understand the needs of a customer who is confused about your organization's products or services, you may have to ask many questions and restate what he or she has said to make sure you have heard all the information accurately.

cont'd

Even when you are certain that you understand, it is critical to restate, so that *customers* know that you understand. Empathize with their point of view, then restate to show and assure them that, indeed, you do understand what they need and why it is important to them.

Connecting: asking effective questions – skill overview

The information we get from our customers is only as good as the questions we ask them. The key is knowing how to construct questions that will uncover important information about customers' needs. There are three kinds of questions; each designed to obtain specific types of information from customers.

Closed questions

Closed questions are used to obtain or confirm specific facts. They are mostly used in fast-moving, uncomplicated interactions with customers and elicit brief responses. They usually begin with 'Is...?', 'Do...?', 'Can...?', 'How many...?' or 'Who...?'. For example:

- 'When would you like it delivered?'
- 'Do you know who your consultant is?'
- 'Was the number easy to find?'
- 'When do you need it?'

Open questions

Open questions are used to elicit more information from the customer. They are mainly used in complex situations, in which the customer's need may be unclear or in which many choices are available. They usually begin with 'Who...?', 'What...?', 'Where...?', or 'Why...?'. For example:

- 'What kind of service are you looking for?'
- 'How can I help you with those applications?'
- 'When does the problem occur?'
- 'How do you use the report?'

High-gain questions

These are open questions that encourage the customer to evaluate, analyse, speculate or express feelings. They usually begin with 'What...?', 'If...?', 'Suppose...?', or 'How...?'. For example:

- 'What are the three most important things I could do to work with you on this?'
- 'How would you compare our service with that of other suppliers?'
- 'How would you like us to resolve this situation?'

Connecting: worksheet – writing high-gain questions

Purpose

This exercise gives you an opportunity to formulate some high-gain questions that you can use with your customers.

Instructions

In the spaces below, write two or three high-gain questions that you could use with a selected customer. Target your questions on uncovering the customer's needs, determining his or her level of satisfaction with your organization's products or services, or examining any other topic that is relevant.

High-gain question 1:

High-gain question 2:

High-gain question 3:

13 Customer skills 4: setting expectations

Summary
Participants work in small groups or pairs to discover the overt and covert expectations inherent in any customer interaction. They then present their conclusions.

Purpose
To learn and review the skills of offering information, options and managing expectations.

Format
Pairs or small groups.

Type
Skill-builder.

Suitable for
All levels of customer service staff.

Resources
Copies of the two handouts for each participant.

Time
35–45 minutes.

Procedure
1. Introduce the exercise by stating the purpose set out above.
2. Stress the importance of managing and setting expectations – give everyday examples, such as notification of train timetable delays, returning telephone calls, and so on.
3. Distribute copies of the two handouts – 'Setting expectations' and 'Options and expectations worksheet' – to each participant.
4. Next, ask the participants to work in pairs or small groups and prepare a three-minute presentation on a chosen situation and its solution(s). Allow 20 minutes for this.
5. Monitor the groups and provide input as required.
6. Ask each group to present, in turn.
7. Run a brief discussion on the learning points.

Options

- List the key points and display on flipchart pages.
- Give specific expectations and examples, such as the speed of response expected by the customer, delivery time required, action required and the customer's expectation of customer service staff.

Setting expectations

In this exercise, you work with a partner or small group to discuss and apply the skills of offering information and options, setting expectations, and getting agreement. The exercise gives you a preview of how you might use these helping skills in your job.

Instructions

- **Step 1**
  Imagine an actual work situation in which you need to use helping skills – that is, offering information and options, setting expectations and getting agreement.
- **Step 2**
  Briefly describe your situation to your group members. Select one member's situation to discuss in greater depth. Notify the trainer of the situation you select.
- **Step 3**
  Ask what the customer expected in the situation and what the provider could do and could not do to meet those expectations. Record your thoughts. You may wish to use the 'Options and expectations worksheet' to help you think through the situation and prepare a solution.
- **Step 4**
  Prepare a three-minute presentation of your chosen situation and its solution(s). You may present in any way you wish. For example, you might present a brief role play or short report to the whole group. Your presentation should show how you would offer options and set expectations.

You have 20 minutes to discuss your situation and prepare your presentation.

Setting expectations: options and expectations worksheet

Customer:

Service provider:

Customer situation:

Specific customer requirements/ priorities	Information (about your products or services)	Options (to address customer needs)

Expectations to set with your customer

What you can do	What you cannot do

Summary: setting expectations

- Offering information and options increases customer involvement and satisfaction.
- Setting realistic expectations increases your chances of meeting or exceeding them.
- Getting agreement confirms the next steps for the provider and customer.

14 Customer survey form

Summary
Working in small groups, participants review a variety of customer feedback or survey forms, before working to design and create their own form.

Purpose
To encourage a focus on the ten most important measures of satisfaction for the organization's customers.

Format
Small groups.

Type
Improving methods.

Suitable for
All levels of customer service staff, including managers and supervisors.
A selection of customer survey forms.

Resources
A copy of the handout for each participant.
Pens and paper.
A flipchart and marker pens.

Time
45–60 minutes.

Procedure
1. In advance, collect about a dozen sample customer survey forms and questionnaires from a variety of businesses and for various purposes.
2. Introduce the activity by stating the purpose set out above.
3. Distribute a copy of the handout and the sample customer survey forms to each participant.
4. Briefly discuss and highlight the varying approaches – scoring systems, comments, visual design techniques, wording and so forth.
5. Divide the participants into small groups of 3–6.
6. Explain the task and set a nominal time of 20–30 minutes. Make sure that everyone has a supply of pens and paper.

7. Once the time is up, or when all groups have finished, ask each group to present their survey form/questionnaire, using a flipchart if appropriate.

Variation   Task different groups with varying requirements – for example, a customer interview survey, face-to-face interview, postal survey, point-of-sale type card, focus group questions.

Customer survey form: assignment

The purpose of this activity is to focus attention on the factors that are important to customers by designing a usable customer service questionnaire or form. Working in your groups, please:

1. Review the sample customer survey forms provided, and use these to stimulate initial ideas.

2. Make a list of the ten most important measures of satisfaction – from the customer's viewpoint – *for your organization.*

3. Create a series of questions that might be used on a form or in conversation to test customer satisfaction for each of the ten measures.

4. Produce a draft survey form or questionnaire.

5. Be prepared to present your survey form or questionnaire back to the group and explain how you have selected the questions and layout you have used.

15   Defining excellent customer service

Summary   Working in small groups, participants identify strategies to produce good customer service.

Purpose   To focus on different levels of service and identify the key elements or actions that produce *delighted*, *satisfied* and *dissatisfied* customers.

Format   Small groups.

Type   Subject breaker.

Suitable for   All levels of customer service staff.

Resources   A copy of the handout for each participant.
A flipchart and marker pens.

Time   20–25 minutes or as required.

Procedure   1.   Distribute a copy of the handout to each participant.
2.   Introduce the activity by presenting and discussing the definitions of *delighted*, *satisfied* and *dissatisfied* customers as stated on the handout, perhaps using some examples drawn from your own experience.
3.   Form the participants into groups of 3–7.
4.   Explain that each group should identify some actions or strategies that relate to each of the three customer experiences, using real-life examples where possible and based on their own organization, products or services.
5.   Ask the participants to prepare flipchart pages for review in the whole group.
6.   Allow 10–15 minutes (or longer) for the groups to generate as many ideas as possible.

7. Reconvene the main group in a circle around the flipchart.
8. Post up one page at a time and review the key points.

Variations

- Focus on generic examples common to the participants' experience – for instance, holidays, hotels, shops, business services and so on.
- Focus on one aspect of service – for example, handling complaints, telephone skills and so forth.

Defining excellent customer service

Definitions

- *Delighted* customers are those whose experience exceeds their conscious or unconscious expectation.
- *Satisfied* customers are those whose experience equals their expectation.
- *Dissatisfied* customers are those whose experience is less than their expectation.

Task

Working in your group identify some actions or strategies that relate to each of the three customer experiences, using real-life examples where possible and based on your own organization, products or services. Transfer your notes onto flipchart paper.

Delight	Satisfaction	Dissatisfaction

16   Gap analysis

Summary   Working in small groups, participants research and reflect on the gaps between their current level of service and what is expected.

Purpose   To determine the gap between current service provision and customer expectation.

Format   Small groups.

Type   Ice-breaker/energizer.

Suitable for   All levels of customer service staff.

Resources   Copies of the two handouts for each participant.

Time   20 minutes.

Procedure
1. Introduce activity by stating the purpose set out above and distribute copies of the two handouts to each participant.
2. Organize the participants into groups of 4–5 and ask them to work carefully through the task. Allow 10 minutes for this.
3. Share and discuss the results.

Options   Ask the participants to visit, or talk with, at least three customers before the training session or meeting to determine what they expect for each of your listed product or service outputs, how important each expectation is, and how the customers rate your company in providing it.

Gap analysis 1

To determine the gaps between what you do and what your customers expect, complete the following analysis using handout 2.

1. Write down your four most important outputs (products or services) in the spaces indicated.

2. Either use your own judgement or visit or talk with at least three customers to determine what they expect for each of your listed product or service outputs, how important each expectation is, and how they rate your company in providing it.

3. Fill in what you have concluded or learnt about your customers and their expectations for each product or service listed.

4. Note how important each expectation is to the customer on the following scale:
   - 1 = unimportant/unnecessary
   - 2 = somewhat important
   - 3 = very important.

5. Indicate how your customers rate your product or service in this area on the following scale:
   - 1 = does not meet expectations
   - 2 = meets expectations adequately
   - 3 = exceeds expectations.

Gap analysis 2

A: Product/service: _____

Expectation	Importance	Rating

B: Product/service: _____

Expectation	Importance	Rating

C: Product/service: _____

Expectation	Importance	Rating

D: Product/service: _____

Expectation	Importance	Rating

17 Happy customer/ unhappy customer 1

Summary	Working in pairs or small groups, participants use their real-life experiences to identify specific elements common to 'unhappy' customer situations.
Purpose	To highlight some key qualities and characteristics in successful customer service delivery.
Format	Pairs or small groups.
Type	Key point/energizer.
Suitable for	All levels and types of customer service staff, especially front-line staff.
Resources	Paper and pens. A flipchart and marker pens or OHP.
Time	45 minutes.
Procedure	*This activity can be used to introduce any skill-based activity or discussion on customer service skills, not just as a course introduction or ice-breaker.*

1. Explain that, in this activity, you are going to recall a successful customer experience, try to identify why it was successful, and then see if there are any common elements across the group.
2. Write the phrase 'Happy Customers' on a flipchart in large letters.
3. Next, ask the participants to work in pairs or small groups and to recall their 'best customer' stories. They should make some notes on the event, identifying some of the reasons

why they think the customer was satisfied and assessing its particular personal significance.

4. After about 15 minutes, or when most people have finished, reconvene the whole group and invite each pair or group in turn to recall their tale (about 2–3 minutes each).

5. As the participants describe their experiences, identify key elements and contributing factors and post them on a flipchart or OHP.

6. If the participants offer any vague explanations, such as 'a very nice person' or 'an easy-to-please customer' try to identify some key skills or behaviours that may have contributed by questioning further. Often, a good way of doing this is to ask the participants to recall the event step-by-step, making sure that they don't generalize any important elements.

7. Thank the participants for their input and record any final key points.

You might like to start or end the activity by recalling a particularly memorable customer event of your own.

18 Happy customer/ unhappy customer 2

Summary Working in pairs or small groups, participants use their real-life experiences to identify specific elements common to 'happy' customer situations.

Purpose To highlight some key qualities and characteristics in successful service delivery.

Format Pairs or small groups.

Type Key point/energizer.

Suitable for All levels and types of customer service staff, especially front-line staff.

Resources Paper and pens.
A copy of the handout for each participant.
A flipchart and marker pens or OHP.

Time 45–50 minutes.

Procedure *This activity can be combined with the previous one to create a larger activity that explores or contrasts the differences between successful and less successful sales calls or customers. It can also be used to introduce any skill-based activity or discussion on customer service skills, not just as a course introduction or ice-breaker.*

1. Introduce the activity by asking the participants why some customers are *less* satisfied than others.
2. Explain that, in this activity, they are going to recall a lost or unsatisfied customer, try to identify why, and then see if there are any common elements across the group. Be sure to emphasize that this is not an exercise in laying blame or

making people feel inadequate, but rather an objective look to see what can be learned and applied in the future. *You might like to start the activity by recalling a particularly embarrassing experience of your own. After giving a short overview and description, ask participants why they think the sale or customer might have been such a flop.*

3. Write the phrase 'Unhappy Customers' on the flipchart.
4. Next, ask the participants to work in pairs or small groups and to recall their 'worst customer' stories. They should make some notes on the event, identifying some of the reasons why the sale was unsuccessful and assessing its particular personal significance.
5. After about 15 minutes, or when most people have finished, reconvene the whole group and invite each pair or group in turn to recall their tale (about 2–3 minutes each).
6. As the participants describe their experiences, identify key elements and contributing factors and post them on a flipchart or OHP. A typical list might include:

   ● Lack of skill
   ● Too rushed
   ● Didn't listen; talked too much
   ● Poor preparation; unqualified customer
   ● Didn't believe in product
   ● Poor product knowledge
   ● Lack of rapport with customer.

7. If the participants offer any vague explanations, such as 'luck' or 'customer just wasn't interested', try to identify some key skills or behaviours that may have contributed by questioning further. Often, a good way of doing this is to ask the participants to recall the event step-by-step, making sure that they don't generalize any important elements.
8. Distribute a copy of the handout to each participant and ask them to make a list of positive action points that they can use in the future to apply any lessons learned. Emphasize that they should finish the exercise with a set of *action* points – things to do differently next time – rather than a list of things that they have done wrong. Allow 5 minutes for this task.
9. Thank the participants for their input and record any final key points that have emerged.

Happy customer/unhappy customer 2: action plan

The most important things that I have learned from this session are:

How I can use these to improve my service skills:

Other key ideas to implement:

Actions	By when/how

19 Improving customer service

Summary   This activity can be used to review internal or external customer service standards and procedures.

Purpose   Participants work in small groups to brainstorm the changing needs of customers. The whole group then discusses the results.

Format   Small groups.

Type   Discussion forum/problem solving.

Suitable for   All levels of customer service staff.

Resources   A flipchart and marker pens or OHP (optional).
A copy of the handout for each participant.

Time   30–45 minutes.

Procedure
1. Before the start of the activity, draw a chart on a flipchart containing the points set out on the handout.
2. Lead a short discussion or presentation on how customer service expectations and demands are changing all the time. Explain that this activity will allow the participants to identify what these expectations are and begin to understand how they can be improved.
3. Organize the participants into small groups and distribute a copy of the handout to each participant and ask them to work in their groups to work through the items. Allow 15–20 minutes.
4. After all the groups have completed the task, collect the handouts from each group.
5. Either collate the points and ideas away from the session (perhaps during a break) and present back later, or simply

list the points collectively on some flipchart pages or OHP foils for the whole group to review. Either way, these ideas should ideally be kept and reviewed later.

Variations   Develop your own checklist of service questions for groups to work through.

Improving customer service: what are your service standards?

1. Have you defined a level of service that you strive to deliver? If not, develop standards for the following:

How quickly you should return telephone calls	
How closely you should monitor the timely delivery of products or services	
How often you should keep in touch with customers and prospects	
How frequently you should solicit customer feedback on your products and service quality	
Any other aspects of service which you can add to this list	

2. List three ways to make it easier for customers to do business with your company.
    a.
    b.
    c.

3. List three ways to streamline the problem-solving process for customers.
    a.
    b.
    c.

cont'd

4. List three ways to reduce or eliminate any recurring problems that your customers experience with your product or services.

   a.

   b.

   c.

5. What opportunities are presented by the recurring problems that you listed in question 4? How can you turn unhappy customers into loyal customers?

Reproduced from *Customer Service Games for Training*, Graham Roberts-Phelps, Gower, Aldershot

20 Integrating products and services

Summary   Working in small groups, participants brainstorm ideas for adding customer service value to a simple product.

Purpose   To help participants reflect on the intangibles of customer service and how to improve or increase them.

Format   Small groups.

Type   Key point.

Suitable for   All levels, especially managers and marketing staff.

Resources   A copy of the handout for each group.

Time   30–40 minutes.

Procedure   1.   Introduce the activity by discussing an example in which, unusually, customer satisfaction – good, bad or indifferent – is based on a total experience, not just one aspect. For example, in servicing a car, it is not just the mechanical competence of the staff, but their politeness and helpfulness, their ability to book the date and time you want, having the car ready at the time promised and any extras the company can dream up – valet, courtesy car, and so on – that makes the difference.
2.   Organize the participants into groups of four or more. Give each group a copy of the handout.
3.   Ask each group to brainstorm as many strategies as they can for differentiating one of the following products:

- Paper clips
- Computer disks

- Insurance
- Twelve-ounce beverage cans
- Natural gas
- Package delivery
- Their business.

4. State that they may not change the product itself; they should, instead, focus on the integrated product, such as delivery, customer relationship, billing, references, and value-added features. Allow 20–30 minutes.
5. Ask the groups to present back to the whole group once time is up.

Integrating products and services

1. Brainstorm as many strategies as you can for differentiating one of the following products:

   - Paper clips
   - Computer disks
   - Insurance
   - Twelve-ounce beverage cans
   - Natural gas
   - Package delivery
   - Your business

2. You may not change the product itself; instead, focus on the integrated product, such as delivery, customer relationship, billing, references and value-added features.
3. When you have finished generating ideas, look over the list and try to find something useful, or something to improve on, for each suggestion.

21   Key telephone skills

Summary   Participants work in small groups to brainstorm the basic dos and don'ts of good telephone behaviour.

Purpose   To help weed out bad habits and remind everyone of the basics.

Format   Pairs or small groups.

Type   Key point.

Suitable for   All levels and types of customer service staff, especially telephone staff.

Resources   Copies of the two handouts for each participant.
A flipchart and marker pens or OHP.

Time   20–30 minutes or as required.

Procedure   *This is a useful review activity after a training video, demonstration, or as a refresher training session following on from a previous course.*

1. Divide the participants into pairs or groups of three and distribute a copy of the handout 'Key telephone skills: dos and don'ts' to each participant.
2. Ask the participants to complete their own dos and don'ts on *all* aspects of serving or selling to customers by telephone. Under the dos they should list the things that impress them and they like to hear or have found effective and successful. Under the don'ts they should enter all the things that annoy them, don't work or sound unprofessional. Ask them to imagine that they are teaching someone how to use the telephone for the first time.
3. After about 15 minutes, or when most people have finished, ask each group to elect a spokesperson to present their dos

and don'ts using a flipchart or OHP slides. Allow a further 5 minutes for preparation of their presentation notes.

4. At the end of each presentation ask if any other participants have any questions.

5. Next, ask the participants to make a note of any key points presented that they didn't have. Discuss any points arising, if you consider it appropriate.

6. Conclude the activity by summarizing the key points using the 'Key telephone skills: notes' handout, adding your own suggestions and examples. Thank the participants for their contribution and distribute a copy of the 'Key telephone skills: notes' for future reference.

Discussion points

- What are the things that others do or don't do on the telephone that annoy you most?

- How can you avoid such things as passing a caller around, holding for too long, incomplete message taking and so forth?

Option   Agree a list of actions for helping to ensure that the dos are carried out and the don'ts avoided.

Key telephone skills: dos and don'ts

Using the two columns below, complete your own list of dos and dont's on **all** aspects of professional telephone skills, for both inbound and outbound calls.

Dos	Don'ts

Reproduced from *Customer Service Games for Training*, Graham Roberts-Phelps, Gower, Aldershot

Key telephone skills: notes

Here are some suggested or sample responses.

Do	Don't
Take the caller's name early	Forget who you are talking to
Use their name often	Become distracted by people/things around you
Smile while you dial!	Eat, drink or chew while on the telephone
Set goals for sales calls	
Have an objective for your goal	Sound like a robot
Stay in control by asking questions	Sound depressed
Take notes whilst on the telephone	Let the customer take control of the call
Pay attention and show that you are listening	Talk for more than 15 seconds without asking a question
Be sincere	Talk more than the customer
Use open questions to build the conversation	Talk too fast
Use closed questions to confirm and show understanding	Insult the customer by interrupting
Be enthusiastic	Slouch in your seat
Be friendly	Be abrupt, rude or sarcastic
Sound alert	Use slang, clichés or repeat the same words or phrases
Adjust your voice to suit that of the other person, in terms of speed, pace, volume, tone, accent and pauses	Put people on hold without asking their permission
Know how to use your telephone – hold, transfer, and so on.	Put people on hold for longer than 30 seconds without going back to them
Answer within 3–5 rings	Cover the mouthpiece to talk to someone else – use the hold button
Say 'please' and 'thank you'	Assume anything – check for understanding
Give information clearly	
Summarize what has been agreed at the end of the call	Put the telephone down before the customer does

22   Mystery shopper

Summary   Participants act as 'mystery shoppers' on other businesses or competitors. These can either be selected for participants or chosen at random. The telephone exercise works best if it is recorded and reviewed. This can be acheived simply by using a loud-speaker telephone and an ordinary cassette recorder placed next to it.

    The retail exercise is obviously only practical if such businesses are nearby. Interesting comparisons and contrasts can often be found by surveying a mix of businesses – large chains, independent businesses and so on.

Purpose   To both virtually and physically take on the customer's perspective and to consciously consider the elements of customer satisfaction that might often only be considered unconsciously.

Format   Pairs or small groups.

Type   Subject breaker.

Suitable for   Customer service staff – supervisors and managers.

Resources   A copy of the relevant handout for each participant.
A flipchart and marker pens.
For the telephone exercise: a speaker telephone and a cassette recorder.

Time   50–60 minutes for the telephone study. 60–75 minutes for the retail study.

Procedure
1. Explain that participants will be asked to work in pairs or groups and actually survey a real business as if they were customers.
2. Organize the participants into pairs or small groups and

distribute a copy of either the 'Telephone' or 'Retail' handout, according to which survey is being carried out.

3. Explain that the participants should work first on listing the elements that they will be using to assess and critique their experiences. Allow about 10 minutes.

4. Next, groups should move on to conduct their mystery shoppers exercise, making notes during and after each telephone call or visit. Allow about 20 minutes for the telephone exercise or until or groups have finished. Only one participant per group needs to make the actual telephone call.

5. When most groups have finished, reconvene and ask each group to present their comments and experiences in turn. Discuss any points and ask for feedback from the other groups. Make sure that all the groups contribute.

6. Summarize the key points on a flipchart.

7. Conclude the activity by reviewing and summarizing the main points from the discussion and thank the participants for their contributions.

Mystery shopper: telephone

Contact, by telephone, two businesses that are not known to you and for which you have some knowledge of the product or service they can provide. Be an interested customer – asking questions, prompting for more information. Test them out as best you can.

Make detailed notes on the aspects of your experience during the telephone conversation. Pay particular attention to:

- The initial greeting, speed of answer and so forth
- The salesperson's connecting skills
- What personal information you gave
- What questions were asked by the salesperson
- Your first impressions
- The knowledge level and manner of the person who dealt with you
- How well they established your needs
- Voice tone and manner
- Product knowledge.

Make detailed notes on each experience. Be sure to comment equally on good and bad aspects or observations that you might have had.

Reproduced from *Customer Service Games for Training*, Graham Roberts-Phelps, Gower, Aldershot

Mystery shopper: retail

Visit two or more businesses near your location. Ask to be shown around the business or discuss product/service offerings in detail. Pretend to be a serious customer enquiry. Make detailed notes on the aspects of your business experience, focusing on the elements you feel most important – possibly one or all of the following:

- How well did they use questions to identify what was important to you?
- How well did they link your needs to the product features and benefits?
- How well did they discuss features and benefits?
- How well did they maintain your interest and attention?
- How well did they handle your questions and objections?

Be sure to comment equally on any good and bad aspects or observations you may have had. How did the businesses compare with one another or even your organization?

23   Personal qualities

Summary   Participants work in pairs or small groups to brainstorm and then debate the top ten personal qualities essential for good service delivery.

Purpose   For participants to recognize that they already have most of the qualities essential to good customer service, that they should use these qualities and that the most important, underlying quality is 'attitude'.

Format   Pairs or small groups.

Type   Subject breaker.

Suitable for   All customer service staff, especially supervisors and managers.

Resources   A copy of the handout for each participant.
                   A flipchart and marker pens.

Time   30–40 minutes.

Procedure   1. Explain that participants will be asked to work in pairs or groups and list the key personal qualities that are needed for an individual to be successful in creating high levels of customer satisfaction.
                   2. Next, organize the participants into pairs or small groups and distribute a copy of the handout to each participant. Explain that they should work on the list for about ten minutes, after which time they should begin to put them in order of priority. They should aim to identify at least ten qualities. Allow about 20 minutes in total for this task.
                   3. When most groups have finished, reconvene the whole group and ask each small group or pair to present their lists in turn. Discuss any points and ask for feedback from the

other groups. Make sure that all the groups contribute. Summarize the key points on a flipchart.

4. Conclude the activity by reviewing and summarizing the main points from the discussion and thank the participants for their contributions.

Discussion points

- Which qualities are skills and which are attitudes?

- How many of these qualities do you already have? Which ones surprise you?

- What conclusions do you draw for your approach to recruiting and training new customer service team members?

Personal qualities

1. Compile a list of at least ten personal qualities which you consider essential to being successful for good service delivery. Then prioritize the list.

Personal qualities	Priority
1.	
2.	
3.	
4.	
5.	
6.	
7.	
8.	
9.	
10.	

2. Be prepared to justify your selections and the order of priority, exploring the views of the other groups.
3. Select an individual from the group who will present your views on the conclusions reached - with comments on points of significance as seen by the group, and a broad view of what was gained from the discussions by the members of the group.

24   Phoney phrases

Summary   Participants work in pairs or small groups to identify unhelpful or insincere phrases or expressions that customers hear repeatedly on the telephone and replace them with better alternatives.

Purpose   To raise awareness about the negative or off-putting expressions that may have become unconscious habits and are detrimental to good customer service.

Format   Pairs or small groups.

Type   Ice-breaker/energizer.

Suitable for   All levels of customer service staff.

Resources   A copy of the handout for each participant.

Time   15 minutes.

Procedure
1. Introduce the activity by stating the purpose set out above.
2. Distribute a copy of the handout to each participant. Organize the participants into pairs or small groups and ask them to write an alternative phrase or expression in the left-hand column. Allow about 5 minutes.
3. Reconvene the whole group and ask the pairs or small groups to review their answers in turn.

Phoney phrases: telephone skills worksheet

The following phrases and expressions are frequently used on the telephone, even though they are not very 'user friendly'. Working in pairs or small groups, write an improved version of each in the right-hand column. Finally, add two more unhelpful or negative phrases that you have heard as a customer.

Expression	Better alternative
What's the problem?	
You ought to….	
The system's down.	
I don't know what you mean by that.	
No, I can't help you.	
You need to talk to someone else.	
Hold, please.	
I can't do anything about it. This is our organization's policy.	
What did you say?	
I can't understand you.	
I'm afraid my manager is in a meeting at the moment.	
It's not my responsibility.	
We don't handle that here.	

cont'd

Expression	Better alternative
You have come through to the wrong extension.	
I haven't a clue.	
There's nothing I can do.	
I'd advise you to….	

25 Presenting ideas for change

Summary Participants work in small groups to brainstorm new ideas. They then take one idea, develop it and present it in the form of a plan for change.

Purpose To identify and suggest ideas for improving customer service delivery.

Format Small groups.

Type Analysis.

Suitable for Managers, supervisors, team leaders, marketing and sales staff.

Resources Copies of the two handouts for each participant.

Time 60–70 minutes.

Procedure
1. State the purpose of the activity as described above and explain that it is often easy to think of ideas to improve customer service, but suggesting them or making them happen is much more difficult.
2. Explain that this activity will give participants a structured approach to packaging and presenting ideas for change.
3. Distribute copies of the two handouts – 'Summary' and 'Assignment' to each participant and ask them to read them through.
4. Next, divide the participants into smaller groups of 3–4 and ask them to complete the assignment. Allow 30–45 minutes.
5. Ask each group to present in turn.
6. Conclude the activity by summarizing each group's plan in turn.

Notes   The stages suggested on the handout are:

1. State the benefits to the organization of your idea. Be able to 'prove' these benefits.
2. Articulate examples of the problem which your idea solves. Explain what the problem 'costs' (not just money but also in terms of customer goodwill, lost customers and so forth).
3. Give a clear definition/explanation of your solution/idea.
4. Anticipate objections and questions.

Presenting ideas for change: summary

How to question policies that create customer problems

1. Find out why the policy or procedure is set that way.
2. Count the cost to the organization: carry out research on the consequences of poor service – that is, how much time and effort is wasted sorting out problems and dissatisfied customers – using common data: sales returns, discounts and so on.
3. Present a reasonably valid 'worst case' that produces a nice big number – that is, a compelling reason for investing in customer service initiatives.
4. Put it in writing.

Your proposal document

Part 1: State your commitment to the end result – the big picture:

- Cover the benefits to all involved.
- Restate mission statements, goals, and so forth.
- Explain why it concerns you personally.

Part 2: Describe the problem. Give:

- Stories and case studies
- Facts and figures
- The bottom-line cost.

Part 3: Describe what needs to be done:

- Be specific.
- Counter doubts and concerns.
- Show the value.
- Set criteria and an action plan.

Reproduced from *Customer Service Games for Training*, Graham Roberts-Phelps, Gower, Aldershot

Presenting ideas for change: assignment

1. First, brainstorm or list a number of different ideas within your group, aiming to achieve a list of ten.
2. Next, choose an idea that you think would give **measurable benefits** to your organization and provide clear improvements to customer service, retention and so forth.
3. Clarify that idea in terms of the points below and develop a short presentation.
4. Present when asked.

Benefits

How you can prove this benefit is important:

Examples of the problem

Calculate the cost:

Your proposed solution

Doubts and concerns that will need to be handled:

26 Questionnaires and ratings

Summary This is a collection of quizzes and questionnaires that can be used in a variety of ways. Participants work on them individually and then review their answers in small groups. Finally, each group presents their conclusions to the other participants.

Purpose Depending on the questionnaire used, to introduce a topic through assessing of personal strengths to strategic planning.

Format Individual and small groups.

Type Key point.

Suitable for All levels of customer service staff.

Resources A copy of the selected handout for each participant.

Time 30–60 minutes, depending on the questionnaire.

Procedure
1. Introduce each questionnaire or quiz activity by stating the objective – that is, to make a detailed conscious assessment of behaviours, skills or attitudes that may be performed automatically or held unconsciously in the workplace.
2. Give each participant a copy of the selected handout or questionnaire and ask them to work on it individually. Set a time limit for completion – say, 5–10 minutes.
3. Next, organize the participants into small groups and ask them to work on flipchart paper to compare and review their answers collectively. For example, they can consider which three elements scored the highest, which scored the lowest and any similarities or variances. Allow 10–20 minutes for this task, depending on the questionnaire.

4. When the time has elapsed, reconvene the whole group and ask each small group to present back their conclusions and notes in a short presentation.

With the true/false questionnaires please use your own viewpoint and judgement to decide which statement is true or false. You may choose to allow the group consensus to decide. The purpose of using such a handout is to facilitate informed and structured debate.

Telephone skills self-assessment 1

Please complete the following questionnaire, as honestly and accurately as you can. Rate your response to each statement on the following scale:

1 = never; 2 = sometimes; 3 = usually; 4 = often; 5 = always.

1. I keep an accurate tracking system to remember callbacks and follow-up calls.	1–2–3–4–5
2. I keep brief but useful notes after each call.	1–2–3–4–5
3. I make sure that I start each call with a clear friendly greeting and my name or department.	1–2–3–4–5
4. I ask people to spell out names, numbers and unusual words.	1–2–3–4–5
5. I repeat back the other person's message to show understanding.	1–2–3–4–5
6. I show active listening on the telephone by acknowledging and repeating key information or phrases.	1–2–3–4–5
7. I use open questions to gather information and control the call.	1–2–3–4–5
8. I use closed questions to gain agreement, confirmation and to summarize.	1–2–3–4–5
9. I make sure that I listen twice as much as I talk.	1–2–3–4–5
10. I focus on achieving my objectives and not discussing too much detail.	1–2–3–4–5
11. I consciously change my voice to sound more confident and professional.	1–2–3–4–5

cont'd

Reproduced from *Customer Service Games for Training*, Graham Roberts-Phelps, Gower, Aldershot

12.	I have prepared answers for all commonly presented objections and questions.	1–2–3–4–5
13.	I use features and benefits to create buying interest and desire.	1–2–3–4–5
14.	I follow up messages and enquiries quickly and professionally.	1–2–3–4–5
15.	I speak more slowly on the telephone, and take more care with my words.	1–2–3–4–5
16.	I handle secretaries and assistants effectively.	1–2–3–4–5
17.	I set clear weekly activity schedules and activity goals.	1–2–3–4–5
18.	I avoid being distracted by other people and things around me.	1–2–3–4–5
19.	I take notes whilst talking to aid concentration and as a record of the call.	1–2–3–4–5
20.	I sound friendly by putting a 'smile' into my voice.	1–2–3–4–5

My score is _____ **out of 200 or** _____ **%.**

Telephone skills self-assessment 2

Please rate your skill in each of the following areas on the following scale:

1 = excellent; 2 = acceptable; 3 = room for improvement.

1.	Preparation and being ready	1–2–3
2.	Responding to an incoming call in a welcoming manner	1–2–3
3.	Making outgoing calls – gaining rapport and quickly establishing the main purpose or intent of the initial enquiry	1–2–3
4.	Creating friendly, confident and credible first impression	1–2–3
5.	Active listening	1–2–3
6.	Asking questions and drawing out	1–2–3
7.	Summarizing and restating	1–2–3
8.	Product knowledge and answering questions	1–2–3
9.	Offering information and using features and benefits	1–2–3
10.	Setting expectations	1–2–3
11.	Bridging to other topics or requirements	1–2–3
12.	Overcoming objections	1–2–3
13.	Closing a call	1–2–3
14.	Paperwork and administration	1–2–3
15.	Motivation and staying positive; making and taking a good number of calls per day	1–2–3

My score is _____ out of 45 or _____ %.

Reproduced from *Customer Service Games for Training*, Graham Roberts-Phelps, Gower, Aldershot

Customer service skills assessment

Please rate your skill in each of the following areas as honestly and accurately as you can. Use the following scale:

1 = extremely skilled – *something you do extremely well*
2 = very skilled
3 = moderately skilled
4 = slightly skilled
5 = not at all – *a real opportunity area!*

	1	2	3	4	5
1. Being ready					
Anticipating the needs of customers; having the information I need or knowing where to get it; having all the equipment I need in working order; competent use of technology; knowing and preparing for times of peak demand.					
2. Welcoming					
Greeting customers and conveying that I am interested and willing to help through tone of voice, verbal language and body language.					
3. Making the call					
Explaining the purpose and benefit of the call and then checking to ensure that the customer understands and agrees to proceed.					
4. Listening					
Hearing and remembering the feelings, facts and the significant concerns that my customers express.					
5. Asking					
Creating effective questions to understand my customers' situations and what they really need; keeping customers participation; controlling the call.					

cont'd

6. Restating	1	2	3	4	5
Letting my customers know that I understand what we have said in terms of both feelings and the facts of the situation; being sure that we agree on what they are asking for.					
7. Offering information and options	1	2	3	4	5
Giving my customers useful information; providing them with choices; using clear explanations and statements; 'packaging' information and options.					
8. Setting expectation and getting agreement	1	2	3	4	5
Letting my customers know what I can and cannot do; being clear; giving specific details.					
9. Exploring further needs and getting agreement	1	2	3	4	5
Asking effective questions; discussing features and benefits to help the customer visualize the usefulness of the service; assessing the agreement level.					
10. Asking for a decision	1	2	3	4	5
Being direct, concise and confident in asking for commitment.					
11. Summarizing and checking	1	2	3	4	5
Summarizing key points and checking for satisfaction.					
12. Thanking	1	2	3	4	5
Expressing appreciation to external and internal customers; making customers feel important.					
13. Following up	1	2	3	4	5
Ensuring that what was promised to my customer is what they received; if passing my customer to other person in the organization, making sure that the transaction is handled smoothly.					

cont'd

14. Handling objections	1	2	3	4	5
Responding to objections stated by my customers; changing an objection into an opportunity.					
15. Handling challenging situations	1	2	3	4	5
Doing my best to understand and help customers who may be angry or upset; recovering from mistakes made by myself or by my organization; giving bad news.					

Three strengths
1.
2.
3.

Three areas for improvement:
1.
2.
3.

Attitude self-assessment

Please complete the following questionnaire as honestly and accurately as you can. Rate your response to each statement on the following scale:

1 = never; 2 = sometimes; 3 = usually; 4 = often; 5 = always

1. When thinking, I say positive, encouraging and helpful words to myself.	1–2–3–4–5
2. I know if I believe I can or believe I cannot do a thing, I am right.	1–2–3–4–5
3. I can differentiate between what I can and cannot do, and I don't worry about them.	1–2–3–4–5
4. I surround myself with similar, positive-minded people.	1–2–3–4–5
5. I focus on ways in which something can be done rather than on problems and obstacles.	1–2–3–4–5
6. I compliment others whenever possible and avoid criticizing them.	1–2–3–4–5
7. I think about my strong points, abilities and reasons for self-worth.	1–2–3–4–5
8. The first thing I say to others, and have them say to me, is something good.	1–2–3–4–5
9. I know that my attitude can make stress positive or negative.	1–2–3–4–5
10. I can't wish a bad day away. I therefore accept it, for it will pass.	1–2–3–4–5
11. I look forward to learning something new every day.	1–2–3–4–5

cont'd

12. I look for, and expect, the best in people. If I am wrong, we still benefit.	1–2–3–4–5
13. I know others can stop me temporarily; I can stop myself permanently.	1–2–3–4–5
14. I eliminate paperwork and red tape in every possible way.	1–2–3–4–5
15. I know that when I blame others I slip further away from improving the situation.	1–2–3–4–5
16. I know that the biggest risk in life is to try to avoid taking risks.	1–2–3–4–5
17. I know that riches usually come not from focusing on riches, but on success.	1–2–3–4–5
18. I know that being afraid of losing something is one sure way to lose it.	1–2–3–4–5
19. I take steps to change problems into results. If I can't, I forget them.	1–2–3–4–5
20. I exercise and rest regularly for a positive attitude, efficiency and energy.	1–2–3–4–5
21. I walk briskly, sit upright, relax and breathe deeply.	1–2–3–4–5
22. I use positive body language to influence myself – I smile.	1–2–3–4–5
23. I make lists of all the positive things I've done, and how I did them.	1–2–3–4–5
24. I truly believe that good things should, can and will happen to me.	1–2–3–4–5
25. I strive to see opportunities in every difficulty and not the reverse.	1–2–3–4–5
26. I set some small goals that I can achieve, then set new ones.	1–2–3–4–5

cont'd

27. I try to be well dressed and groomed because it helps me feel good.	1–2–3–4–5
28. I speak the truth. If I am inclined to lie, I keep silent.	1–2–3–4–5
29. I know that most joy comes from enjoying the work, not reaching for the stars.	1–2–3–4–5
30. I know that to make no decision is often a bad decision.	1–2–3–4–5

My score is _____ out of 150 or _____ %.

Communication self-assessment

Please complete the following questionnaire as honestly and accurately as you can. Rate your response to each statement on the following scale

1 = never; 2 = sometimes; 3 = usually; 4 = often; 5 = always.

1.	I consider the other person's differences when choosing my words.	1–2–3–4–5
2.	I realize that the other person's emotions affect how they receive my words.	1–2–3–4–5
3.	I receive good, friendly feedback to all my communications.	1–2–3–4–5
4.	I use verbal communication to ensure friendly feedback.	1–2–3–4–5
5.	I use written communications for clarity and future reference.	1–2–3–4–5
6.	I use both written and verbal communication when needed.	1–2–3–4–5
7.	I avoid making any assumptions when communicating.	1–2–3–4–5
8.	I avoid blaming others for mistakes in communications.	1–2–3–4–5
9.	I eliminate long words and sentences in my communications.	1–2–3–4–5
10.	I make written communications as warm and friendly as spoken ones.	1–2–3–4–5
11.	In communicating, I focus on my clarity and others' understanding.	1–2–3–4–5

cont'd

12. When communications go wrong, I see what I could have done better.	1–2–3–4–5
13. I stay aware of the other person's body-language and reactions.	1–2–3–4–5
14. I keep everyone fully informed and never leave them in the dark about things.	1–2–3–4–5
15. When I am critical, I end the communication on a positive note.	1–2–3–4–5
16. I often explain something in several different ways to help clarity.	1–2–3–4–5
17. I don't make other person feel stupid when giving feedback.	1–2–3–4–5
18. I consider others' educational and social differences when talking.	1–2–3–4–5
19. I try to 'feed the grapevine' good information.	1–2–3–4–5
20. When upset or angry, I delay any critical communications if I can.	1–2–3–4–5

Customer service: true or false?

Please consider each of the following statements carefully and mark each with an **X** as either true or false.

Statement	True	False
1. The customer is always right		
2. Customers are more understanding because they know that competition is very tight.		
3. People always, or nearly always, buy on price.		
4. Customers are far more cost-conscious and aware than a few years ago.		
5. Unless people receive poor service or bad merchandise, most customers will continue to stay with their current supplier.		
6. The best measure of customer satisfaction is the level of complaints.		
7. Because of increased competition and information, customers are less aware of all the various options that you can offer.		
8. Customer service initiatives are costly and reduce profit margins.		
9. It is difficult to measure whether customer service is appreciated.		
10. A well run organization should already know what its customers want and expect.		
11. In most organizations, good customer service saves money and increases profitability.		
12. A customer that experiences dissatisfaction that is resolved well is more loyal, not less.		

Telephone skills: true or false?

Please consider each of the following statements carefully and mark each with an **X** as either true or false.

Statement	True	False
1. It is best to answer the telephone as quickly as possible.		
2. It is best to start a telephone conversation with a closed question, such as 'Can I help you?' or 'May I help you?'.		
3. You should avoid giving your name as this may encourage the customer to either blame you or ask for you by name next time they call		
4. You should ask for the customer's name early in a telephone call and use it as often as possible.		
5. You should always call customers by their first name as this is more friendly and helpful.		
6. It is best never to keep a customer on hold for more than five minutes.		
7. The limited and artificial nature of the telephone makes it easier to lie or mislead someone.		
8. One minute on the telephone is the equivalent of five or six minutes of face-to-face time.		
9. People don't mind being put on hold so long as the music is good.		
10. It is best to speak quickly on the telephone, because it makes the call as short as possible and you sound confident and professional.		

Training evaluation

On the following scale, please rate the degree to which you believe your service provider(s) has (have) improved on the following since attending your customer service training programme.

5 = very substantial improvement
4 = substantial improvement
3 = moderate improvement
2 = minor improvement
1 = no improvement

	1	2	3	4	5
Receiving					
1. Being emotionally and mentally ready for the customer interaction					
2. Using body language that shows interest and enthusiasm					
3. Using verbal language and tone of voice that engages the customer					
Understanding					
4. Encouraging customer comments and thoughts through active listening					
5. Using high-gain questions to encourage the customer to think, share feelings, evaluate or speculate					
Helping					
6. Involving the customer in generating options for solutions to their needs					

cont'd

	1	2	3	4	5
7. Resisting trying to provide information or 'an answer' until the customer's need or problem is sufficiently understood					
Keeping					
8. Checking with the customer to ensure that their need or concern was met					
9. Clearly summarizing the customer's needs or agreement					
10. Clearly stating a next step					
12. Bridging to future opportunities					
Challenging situations					
13. Encouraging customer complaints rather than getting defensive					
14. Using questioning skills to fully understand the customer issue					
15. Gaining a sufficient understanding of the customer issue before responding with information or action					
Teamwork					
16. Making smooth handovers to co-workers					
Overall assessment					
17. Confidence in ability to interact with customers					
18. Improved customer interactions					
19. Meeting customer expectations					
20. Improved business relationships with customers					

Reproduced from *Customer Service Games for Training*, Graham Roberts-Phelps, Gower, Aldershot

27 Selling the service imperative

Summary   From a starting point of 12 ideas for selling the service imperative, participants work in small groups to identify and action-plan ways of increasing management and staff awareness and buy-in to customer service excellence.

Purpose   To prepare a practical action plan or summary of ideas that can be used to increase the awareness of other staff or managers.

Format   Small groups.

Type   Improving methods.

Suitable for   All levels of customer service staff, especially managers and supervisors.

Resources   Copies of the two handouts for each participant.
A flipchart and marker pens.

Time   40–50 minutes.

Procedure   1.   Introduce the activity by stating the purpose set out above. Emphasize the importance of creating an organization that takes customer satisfaction seriously at all levels.
2.   Explain that, in order to initiate a *customer-driven* culture company-wide, you will need other managers on your side. You literally need their 'buy-in', because they will probably have to pay for the costs of quality service out of their own budgets. So service quality lives and dies on management, staff and other departments' support. If you don't have it, you need to 'sell' your service to them.
3.   Distribute a copy of the handout, 'Summary', to each participant and explain that it lists 12 practical ideas on how

to increase awareness of customer service issues and 'buy-in' from others.

4. Ask the participants to work in small groups to select the three ideas that they consider the best and produce an action plan for each one. Allow 15–20 minutes.
5. Reconvene the whole group and ask each subgroup to present back using a flipchart.
6. Discuss their selection and their action plans.
7. Circulate the handout 'Three ways of gaining support', and allow time for questions.
8. Run a brief discussion on likely obstacles to implementing these ideas and how they might be overcome or avoided.

Selling the service imperative: summary

To initiate a *customer-driven* culture company-wide, you will need other managers on your side. You literally need their 'buy-in', because they will probably have to pay for the costs of quality service out of their own budgets. So service quality lives and dies on management support. If you don't have it, you need to 'sell' your service to them.

Ideas to increase management buy-in

1.	Assess your internal customers' needs. Everyone, including managers, has an internal customer. Find out what your internal customers require of you and your subordinates and make sure that you supply it.
2.	Be a role model yourself for the skills you are advocating. Treat your internal customers very, very well.
3.	Be proactive by sharing information. Don't wait for people to come to you. One good way is to share the customer information you gather. This will often highlight service needs. Take the initiative to suggest to other managers how to meet those needs: don't wait for them to come to you.
4.	Develop a departmental mission statement and a presentation. Develop facts, figures, and give a short presentation on customer-driven service, based on your area of responsibility.
5.	Evaluate your problems, and share the results. This helps you prove the value of service excellence, as well as weed out less successful activities.
6.	Focus on what the organization and customers need, rather than what you need. Your job is to serve customers. But 'Service' is not an end in itself.
7.	Know your organization's mission and objectives. (You can use this as a powerful argument to gain support.)

cont'd

8.	Point out the costs of poor service. You are the expert, so let people know the costs and benefits of your efforts to improve service.
9.	Present certificates of achievement for completing a training and problem-solving programme. These really mean something to most people. They will display them – and remember where they got them.
10.	Publicize your efforts internally. Use bulletin boards, newsletters, and the grapevine to let everyone know what great results are produced.
11.	Share both responsibility and credit. Involve other managers in improving service quality from the outset. When your strategy succeeds, publicize both the results achieved and who helped make them happen.
12.	Show other managers how customer-driven service benefits them. Don't talk features; talk benefits. What's in it for them?
13.	Any ideas of your own?

Selling the service imperative: three ways of gaining support

The onion patch technique

1. Select efforts that are within your span of control but are effective enough to capture the attention of more senior managers.
2. Involve others in your efforts.
3. Share the credit with them.
4. Build a network while you make real improvements.
5. Stay alert to any requests from more senior managers to explain what you're doing.
6. Identify the most likely objections and questions, and have answers ready.

Snowballing

1. Sell one manager on the idea.
2. Show other managers how much their colleagues are chipping in.
3. Ask others to pledge budget or staff if higher management approves a roll-out.
4. Show successful results to top managers.

Tin cupping ('Columbo')

1. Answer 'What's in it for me?'.
2. Make everyone an owner.
3. Provide feedback on progress.
4. Return the favour.

28   Service team solutions

Summary   Working in small groups, participants identify an obstacle to good service and brainstorm ways to overcome it.

Purpose   To focus, in a practical way, on how best to implement new ideas and improvements.

Format   Small groups.

Type   Ice-breaker/energizer.

Suitable for   All levels of customer service staff.

Resources   A flipchart and marker pens.
A copy of the handout for each participant (optional).

Time   20–30 minutes.

Procedure
1. Organize the participants into groups of 3–7.
2. Ask each group to identify a stumbling block or obstacle to good service which they might, or do, encounter. Write these on a flipchart.
3. Next, ask the groups to generate as many ideas for overcoming the obstacle as possible. Encourage them to be as creative or outrageous as they can. Sometimes the most far-fetched ideas are the most successful! They should write their chosen obstacle at the top of a flipchart page and then record their ideas and solutions underneath, as they brainstorm. Allow a minimum of 10 minutes for this.
4. Reconvene the whole group in a circle around the flipchart.
5. Post up one page at a time and review the ideas and suggestions.

Variations and options
- Offer the groups problems or obstacles to resolve that you

have collected earlier. These might include obstacles highlighted during an earlier part of the training course.

- Distribute the handout and ask participants to spend 5 minutes individually listing their own ideas for solutions to a problem or obstacle, before working together in a small group or team. This will illustrate that two heads really are often better than one in this kind of situation.

Service team solutions

1. Identify an obstacle to serving customers well or achieving total customer delight.
2. Take 5 minutes, to individually brainstorm ways to overcome it.

Obstacle

Potential solutions

29   The BIG win!

Summary   Participants work in pairs to allocate an imaginary sum that actually equates to the number of seconds in a day.

Purpose   To open participants' eyes to the value of their time.

Format   Pairs or main group.

Type   Ice-breaker/energizer.

Suitable for   All levels of customer service staff.

Resources   Flipchart and marker pens.

Time   10–15 minutes or as required.

Procedure   1. Write £86,400 in large text on the flipchart.
2. Describe how the group has just won a large prize in the National Lottery as part of a syndicate. The individual prize money is **£86,400 each**. Ask the participants to work in pairs to decide how they are going to spend their money, as well as persuading their partners what they should buy. Under the agreed rules of the syndicate, any money left unspent by the end of the day gets distributed amongst the others. Allow 3–4 minutes and encourage the participants to work quickly.
3. When the time is up, compare the responses on the flipchart and run a short discussion on the most popular or unusal items. Ask the participants whether they notice anything significant about the amount of £86,400?
4. In fact, 86,400 is the number of seconds that we are given at the start of every day. Run a short discussion on the following points.

Discussion points

- If we don't decide how to spend our time, who does?

- Do we ever plan our time as carefully or a thoughtfully as we spent an imaginary £86,400?

- Is time more valuable than money?

- What would you do if you had more time?

30   The invisible sum

Summary   This is a simple brainteaser activity directed by the trainer, in which participants make a calculation using random numbers and are given the correct answer by the trainer!

Purpose   To sharpen thinking.

Format   Main group.

Type   Ice-breaker/energizer.

Suitable for   All levels of customer service staff.

Resources   Pens and paper
A calculator (optional).

Time   10–15 minutes or as required.

Procedure   In this surprising trick you add up four rows of figures without seeing them – and arrive at the correct total! A reference book that gives dates of historical events and of well-known people's birthdays is useful though not essential. It is essential, however, that the participants should be able to do simple arithmetic correctly. A calculator would be useful – as long as it is used carefully. It is vital that the participants get their sums right!

1. Begin by asking the participants to write down the year of birth of any living person, and then to write down the year of any significant event that has happened within the nineteenth and twentieth centuries.
2. Now get them to calculate how many years have passed since this event took place, counting to the end of the present year. After this, let them add 35 to the age the chosen person will be at the end of this year. Finally ask them to total all four numbers.

3. Appear to be adding up the unseen numbers and writing down the total, figure by figure.
4. Give them the solution and enjoy their amazement.

How to do it This effective trick is very easy indeed. The total is always twice the current year plus 35.

Example:	Ian Botham		*b.* 1955
	Indian Mutiny		1857
	Years since event		143
	Age (45) + 35		80
		Total:	4035
		2000 x 2 =	4000
			35
			4035

As you know the answer before you even begin the trick, you have every opportunity to concentrate on its presentation. Try to give the impression that you are actually adding up the invisible figures, aided by some sixth sense.

31 Think of a number

Summary   This is a simple puzzle activity directed by the trainer and useful as an ice-breaker or diversionary energizer.

Purpose   To sharpen thinking.

Format   Main group.

Type   Ice-breaker/energizer.

Suitable for   All levels of customer service staff.

Resources   Paper and pens.

Time   10–15 minutes.

Procedure   1. Point out that three is reputed to be the most magical of all numbers. Ask everyone to: 'Write down any two-figure number you please, then multiply it by three. Next add nine, which is three multiplied by itself. Now multiply the result by three again. Finally add your original number.'
2. Ask the participants to write the final total inside a triangle. This total will be a three-figure number. Then tell them to put a circle round the last two figures. Then with no further information to help you, write down or announce the original chosen number.

Answer – how to do it
1. The encircling of the last two figures is a piece of misdirection to lead people to suppose that you somehow work out the answer from this. In fact you ignore the last figure altogether. The first two figures provide the solution. All you have to do is to subtract 2 from them. For example:

52 x 3 = 156
156 + 9 = 165
165 x 3 = 495
495 + 52 = 547

2. Subtract 2 from the first two figures of the final total and you get the number 52.

*Note: If the chosen double-figure number happens to be 98 or 99, the result will be a four-figure number, and you should subtract 2 from the first **three** figures.*

32 Three-letter words

Summary	This is a short brainteasing activity which encourages participants to work together and can be used to provide a break between sessions.
Purpose	To get participants to work together and use their minds.
Format	Individuals, pairs or small groups.
Type	Ice-breaker/energizer.
Suitable for	All levels of customer service staff.
Resources	A copy of one of the handouts for each participant. Small prizes for the winners.
Time	5 minutes or as required.
Procedure	1. Distribute a copy of one of the handouts to each participant. Ask the participants to work individually, in pairs or small groups to generate as many new words as they can from the original word. Allow about 3 minutes.
	2. Next, ask the participants to read out their answers and award prizes, such as chocolate bars, to the winners.
Variation	Use a term or phrase from your own organization.

Three-letter words 1

Take 3 minutes to see how many three-letter words you can make from the following words:

Customer
Service

Three-letter words 2

Take 3 minutes to see how many three-letter words you can make from the following words:

Happy
Customers

33   What kind of customer are you?

Summary   Participants work individually and then in small groups to reflect on and discuss their own preferences as a customer.

Purpose   To encourage participants to 'put themselves in the customer's shoes'.

Format   Individuals and small groups.

Type   Ice-breaker/energizer.

Suitable for   All levels of customer service staff.

Resources   A copy of the handout for each participant.

Time   20–30 minutes.

Procedure   1. Introduce the activity by stating the purpose set out above.
2. Distribute a copy of the handout to each participant and ask them to complete it, working individually. Allow 5 minutes.
3. Organize the participants into groups of 3–4, scattered around the room or in separate rooms. Ask them to compare their responses with each other, noting any areas of agreement or difference. Allow 10–15 minutes.
4. When the time is up, reconvene the whole group and review the responses by asking for examples. Run a short discussion on some of the characteristics common to our favourite and least favourite suppliers.

What kind of customer are you?

	My favourite is ... (with one reason)	My least favourite is ... (with one reason)
Supermarket		
Clothes shop		
Department store		
Holiday company		
Restaurant		
Coffee shop		

cont'd

	My favourite is ... (with one reason)	My least favourite is ... (with one reason)
Utility provider		
Car manufacturer/ garage		
Airline		

34 What makes customers buy?

Summary   Participants rate a series of options – would they buy a, b, or c? The choices they make illustrate their attitude to the three variables: price, service and quality.

Purpose   To determine how much participants value price, service and quality – and under what circumstances.

Format   Pairs or small groups.

Type   Analysis.

Suitable for Managers, supervisors, team leaders, marketing and sales staff.

Resources   A copy of the handout for each participant.

Time   20–30 minutes.

Procedure   1. Introduce the activity by stating the purpose as described above.
2. Begin by saying that, when we choose the products and services that we need or want as customers, it involves a complex, and usually unconscious, analysis of brand, product features, service and perceptions of value and quality.
3. Distribute the handout and ask the participants to score each question. Allow 5 minutes.
4. Next, divide the participants into smaller groups of 2–3 and ask them to work through each question, discussing their answers. What conclusions can they draw about price, service and quality? Allow 10–15 minutes.
5. Conclude the activity by summarizing the group consensus – which is usually that cost is less important than 'value' and added service.

What makes customers buy?

This exercise will help you determine how much you value price, service and quality – and under what circumstances. Circle the letter beside the purchase you would rather make for each of the following pairs.

1.	C	A 'named brand' margarine @ £2.09	A	Generic margarine @ £1.89
2.	C	Great coffee @ £4.00/lb		Reasonable coffee @ £3.50/lb
3.	C	£100 tyres lasting 12 months	A	£80 tyres lasting 8 months
4.	B	£200 repair taking 1 day	A	£150 repair taking 5 days
5.	C	£90 for an executive hotel room with excellent facilities	A	£70 for a standard hotel room with fewer facilities and less space
6.	B	Retail price for clothes at a store with valet parking, free alterations, gift wrapping, helpful salespeople	A	10 per cent off the same clothes at a self-service store with no amenities
7.	B	A movie on cable with no commercials	A	The movie on 'free' TV two years later with a commercial every 15 minutes
8.	C	A personal computer with numerous features which are difficult to learn	B	A computer costing the same with fewer features and easier to master

cont'd

Reproduced from *Customer Service Games for Training*, Graham Roberts-Phelps, Gower, Aldershot

9.	C	Lunch at a fast-food restaurant with good food and poor service	B	Lunch for the same price with worse food and better service
10.	C	A great book that is difficult to find	B	A good book that you can find at any store
11.	A	A compact disc player costing £119 from a discount store with a bad reputation for repairs	B	The same CD player for £189 from a store with a good reputation for repairs
12.	B	A one-hour photo service of mediocre quality	C	A mail-order photo service that charges the same for better quality

Count up the number of times you have circled each letter:

Total: A _____ B_____ C_____

Interpretation

The more A's you have, the more you value price.
The more B's you have, the more you value service.
The more C's you have, the more you value quality.

Of course, most purchasing decisions are a complex combination of all three of these elements. This exercise serves to highlight the process of choosing between them.

Reproduced from *Customer Service Games for Training*, Graham Roberts-Phelps, Gower, Aldershot

35   What's different about using the telephone?

Summary   Working in small groups, participants reflect on the differences between telephone and other forms of communication.

Purpose   To develop empathy with customers and explore skills, knowledge and attitudes towards service on the telephone.

Format   Small groups.

Type   Ice-breaker/energizer.

Suitable for   All levels of customer service staff.

Resources   Copies of handouts for each participant.

Time   10–15 minutes or as required.

Procedure
1. Organize the participants into small groups of 3–6.
2. Distribute a copy of the handout to each participant.
3. Ask the participants to work as directed on the handout. Encourage everyone to share their ideas as fully as possible – what are the differences and are these good or bad?
4. Allow 10–15 minutes for groups to discuss and note their experiences.
5. Reconvene the whole group and lead a discussion, using the discussion points that follow.

Discussion points

- How significant is the lack of visual communication?

- What is it easier to do on the telephone?

- What is more difficult to do on the telephone?

What's different about using the telephone?

Working as a group, take time to reflect on the question below, making some notes in the space provided.

Be ready to contribute these to the group discussion which will follow. Consider not only your experience in this job, but also in previous ones.

Question: Please consider how using the telephone differs from face-to-face or written communication. Identify at least five differences, with examples.

The difference in telephone communication	Positive/negative examples

36 Who is your customer?

Summary   Participants work in small groups to make spider diagrams of all their customers and discuss their findings.

Purpose   To focus, in a practical way, on the different types of customer that may exist and identify customer value chains and indirect customers. (For example, a hospital might consider that its main 'customer' is the patient receiving treatment. The customer chain might include their friends and relatives. Other customers might include the family or referring doctor, insurance or health care company and so on.)

   This activity is also particularly good for emphasizing 'internal' customer connections.

Format   Small groups.

Type   Subject breaker

Suitable for   All levels of customer service staff.

Resources   Flipchart and marker pens.

Time   20–30 minutes.

Procedure   1. Introduce the activity by presenting and discussing the definitions and examples mentioned under 'Purpose' above.
   2. Organize the participants into groups of 3–7.
   3. Explain that each group should make a spider diagram or mind map all the customers that they serve or add value to as part of their job, using flipchart paper for easy review.
   4. Allow a minimum of 10–15 minutes so that the groups can generate as many ideas as possible.
   5. Reconvene the whole group in a circle around the flipchart.

6. Post up the flipchart sheets one-by-one and review the key points.

Discussion points

- Who is your customer's customer?
- How many levels are there in your 'customer value chain'?
- How does looking at the 'big picture' and considering multiple customers make you feel or look differently at what you do?
- How could you begin to prioritize or group customers together?

37   Who killed the customer?

Summary	Participants work in pairs to reflect on a recent unsuccessful customer service call and draw some conclusions for the future.
Purpose	To focus customer service or sales support staff on areas for improvement.
Format	Pairs.
Type	Ice-breaker/energizer.
Suitable for	All levels of customer service and sales support staff.
Resources	A copy of the handout for each participant. Pens and paper.
Time	30–40 minutes.
Procedure	This activity is based on an exercise that sports people and teams run after each lost game (winning as well, but particularly lost). They review the game or event in detail, analysing each step and trying to piece together the clues as to what happened and why.

1. Introduce the activity as a sort of customer service 'whodunnit'. Using their skills of detection and analysis, the participants are going to try to discover why a particular customer was lost, and what lessons could be learnt.
2. Distribute a copy of the handout to each participant and ask them to work in pairs, selecting one example each and working through the questions as thoroughly as possible. Explain that this should take about 20 minutes (10 minutes for each example).
3. After 20 minutes or so, ask the group to reassemble and go

around the group asking each participant to review their examples and their conclusions, going through each of the four questions in turn.

4. To end the activity, thank the participants for their work and ask them to make a note of any actions they would like to take as a result of what they have just learnt or realized.

Discussion points

- How easy was it to analyse the customer in this way?

- What did you discover by doing this activity?

Who (or what) killed the customer?

The purpose of this exercise is help identify areas for self-development and improvement. Take a moment to select a recent customer that you have lost or were unable to satisfy.

Customer: _____

Brief details:

On a separate sheet of paper, and working with your partner as a prompt, consider the following questions:

- What reasons did the customer give for not going ahead with you?
- What reasons do you believe (honestly) contributed to the call not being successful, or the customer not buying? List all factors that you think apply, giving details and reasons where appropriate.
- If you could wave a magic wand and start the encounter with the customer over again, what would you do differently? (Be as specific and as detailed as you can.)
- What lessons can you learn from this customer that can help in the future?

Be sure to write your comments down and be prepared to present your analysis to the group in a discussion.

Part II

Role plays

38 Role play sessions: customer connecting

Summary	Working in groups of three, participants act out role plays of various customer service situations from selected handouts. Role plays are provided as a series of handouts and case studies. You may also wish to create your own or vary the examples given.
Purpose	Role plays give participants an opportunity to practise using skills of receiving and understanding. The effective use of these skills makes customers feel welcomed and understood.
Format	Groups of three.
Suitable for	All customer service staff.
Resources	**For each group:** One copy of each of the 'Provider' and 'Customer' handouts selected. One copy of the 'Observer' handout. One copy of the 'Sample observation worksheet'. Three copies of the 'Observation worksheet'.
Time	50–60 minutes.
Procedure	1. Explain to the participants that each role play has three roles as follows:

- **Service provider**. The provider has an opportunity to understand the needs of a customer.
- **Customer**. The customer gives the provider as much information as possible, in order to help the provider practise the receiving and understanding skills.
- **Observer**. The observer times the role play, makes notes on the effectiveness of the provider's use of the

receiving and understanding skills, and gives feedback. To prepare, the observer reads the instructions for the observer role on the 'Observer' handout (p. 149)

2. Organize the participants into groups of three. Members of each trio are designated as Participant A, Participant B, or Participant C. There are three rounds in the exercise, so each participant has an opportunity to play each of the three roles, as shown in the chart below.

	Participant A	Participant B	Participant C
Round 1	Service provider	Customer	Observer
Round 2	Observer	Service provider	Customer
Round 3	Customer	Observer	Service provider

3. Give each group copies of the selected role play situations found in the following handouts:

   1. Bank customer and bank provider
   2. Graphic arts department customer and graphic arts department provider
   3. Holiday customer and holiday provider
   4. Apartment rental customer and apartment rental provider
   5. Electronics customer and electronics provider
   6. Restaurant customer and restaurant provider
   7. Help desk customer and help desk provider
   8. Invoiced customer and invoice provider
   9. Contract customer and contract provider
   10. Documentation customer and documentation provider

Also give each group one copy of the 'Observer' handout, one copy of the 'Sample observation worksheet' and three copies of the 'Observation worksheet'.

4. Remind the parcipants that high-gain questions ask the customers to:

   ● Speculate: 'What if...?', 'How about if....?'
   ● Evaluate: 'What exactly..?', 'Specifically...'
   ● React or express feelings.

Timing   Approximate timing for the role plays is as follows:

Select cases: 5 minutes
For each round
Prepare for role: 5 minutes
Role play: 5 minutes
Discussion: 5 minutes
Total: 15 minutes

Trainer's notes: role plays and skills practice

The following role plays are simulated real-life situations which you will be asking participants to act out. The more time you take to create accurate situations and give precise instructions the greater will be the benefit and involvement. Participants will often initially be reluctant to become involved in any form of role play or demonstration, mainly because they are anxious about making mistakes or seeming foolish in front of their colleagues. It is therefore vital that you create a 'safe' environment in which it is alright to ask questions, make mistakes and 'not know' everything.

When you are going to run this type of activity, you should start your training with a participative session-starter or ice-breaker, which encourages the participants to self-disclose in some way to the rest of the group – for example, by relating an embarrassing instance or experience.

It is also important to circulate and share your time and attention around the groups equally. If you are running one main role play in the front of the room, do not make any comments of your own until all the other participants have made their observations.

Giving and receiving feedback

Role play activities involve participants in giving 'feedback' or comment – to the group, to you, or to each other. Giving feedback may be new to many participants, and needs to be done properly if the activity is to achieve its objectives.

Here are some guidelines on giving feedback to share with the participants:

- When giving feedback (or when participants are asked to give feedback), always make sure that your point is clear and concise.
- Use actual and specific examples rather than generalizations.
- Give descriptions, not judgements, and concentrate on aspects of behaviour that can be changed.
- Wait until the recipient is ready and willing to listen (not everybody welcomes feedback – regardless of whether it is good or bad).

147

When receiving feedback (or participants are asked to request feedback), always:

- listen carefully to what is meant (not just said) and check that you have understood the points being made
- avoid being defensive or aggressive in your response and remember that someone else's perceptions are as valid as your own
- choose whether to use the feedback or to ignore it (be selective).

Based on the principle that some people will see a glass of water and describe it as 'half full' and other as 'half empty', be aware that all feedback is subjective and may tell you more about the person giving the answer than the programme itself, or yourself. Therefore, always take a balanced view.

When using feedback forms, always allow participants enough time to fill them in (usually about 2–3 minutes) and make sure that they complete them.

Observer

Role

Your role as observer is very important, because you are watching and listening to the provider to see how well he or she uses the receiving and understanding skills. You are also the timekeeper for the role play.

Timings for each role play are as follows:

- Role preparation: 5 minutes
- Role play: 5 minutes
- Discussion and feedback: 5 minutes.

Preparation

To prepare for the role play, read the customer and provider roles for the round. Review the 'Observation worksheet' that you will complete later.

Tasks

1. Use the 'observation worksheet' to document your observations. Use the 'Sample observation worksheet' as a model.
2. When the role play has concluded, provide feedback, using the following guidelines:

   - Ask the *customer* what the provider did that worked well. Ask for suggestions for improvement.
   - Ask the *provider* what he or she did well and what he or she would improve.

3. Offer any additional feedback you have.

Sample observation worksheet

Did the provider:	Examples
1. Use the *receiving* skills well? • Greet the customer? • Introduce himself or herself and his or her organization? • Speak clearly? • Establish eye contact? Smile? 2. Use the *understanding* skills well? • Listen for, and restate, feelings and facts? • Encourage with eye contact and nodding? • Ask closed questions? • Ask open questions? • Ask high-gain questions? • Summarize by restating facts?	*'Good morning. How may I help you?'* *Friendly tone of voice* *'I understand it's important for you to have reports on time.'* *'How many will be involved?'* *'What's important to you?'*
Advice to provider	
• One thing that worked especially well: • One thing to change:	*Eye contact! It was great!* *Ask more questions. You would have gathered better information on preferences if you had asked more open questions.*

Observation worksheet

Did the provider:	Examples

1. Use the *receiving* skills well?
   ● Greet the customer?
   ● Introduce himself or herself and his or her organization?
   ● Speak clearly?
   ● Establish eye contact? Smile?
 	
2. Use the *understanding* skills well?
   ● Listen for, and restate, feelings and facts?
   ● Encourage with eye contact and nodding?
   ● Ask closed questions?
   ● Ask open questions?
   ● Ask high-gain questions?
   ● Summarize by restating facts?	

Advice to provider	
● One thing that worked especially well: ● One thing to change:	

1: Bank customer

Situation

You have recently moved house to a different area. Now you need a new bank – one that can provide you with a variety of services. You have enjoyed your dealings with your previous bank, but its service deteriorated recently.

Guidelines

This role play gives the provider an opportunity to use his or her skills to gain an understanding of your needs and expectations. Respond to the provider in a natural way.

In role-playing, do not give the provider all the details of your situation or share all the information you have. Wait for the provider to ask you questions. If the provider asks you a closed question, respond with only a brief 'yes' or 'no'. Do not elaborate unless you are asked an open or high-gain question.

In the final part of the role play the provider restates his or her understanding of your needs. The provider does not offer you a solution.

Preparation

1. List some of your requirements for, and expectations of, specific services. Here are some ideas you may wish to consider. Add your own if you wish.

   ● Direct deposit
   ● Safety-deposit box
   ● Interest-earning cheque account.

2. Consider how important this banking service is to you. Decide on the feelings you wish to convey in this interaction.

Reproduced from *Customer Service Games for Training*, Graham Roberts-Phelps, Gower, Aldershot

1: Bank provider

Situation

You are a customer service representative in a bank branch that enjoys an excellent reputation for service. Your responsibilities include helping new customers open accounts. You are quite knowledgeable about the variety of services that your bank offers. You are about to talk to a potential customer who has recently moved to town and is enquiring about your banking services.

Guidelines

You consider yourself as a high-quality provider, and this role play gives you an opportunity to practise welcoming, listening, asking questions and restating the customer's feelings and facts. Focus on obtaining as much information as possible about the customer's needs, wants and expectations.

In framing your questions, take into consideration what your own needs and interests might be, were you the customer in this situation. What questions might you want to be asked?

In the final part of the role play summarize and restate your understanding of the customer's needs. You are not to offer the customer a solution.

Preparation

1. Make a note of what you will say to open the interaction.
2. What needs and expectations might the customer have? Here are some ideas you may wish to consider. Add your own.

   - Cash card/credit card
   - Free banking
   - Savings account.

3. Formulate questions that will help you discover the customer's needs. Use:

   - Closed questions
   - Open questions
   - High-gain questions.

4. Consider what feelings the customer might have?
5. How might you restate those feelings?
6. See the 'Observation worksheet' to review the skills on which the observer will critique you.

Reproduced from *Customer Service Games for Training*, Graham Roberts-Phelps, Gower, Aldershot

2: Graphic arts department customer

Situation

You are an employee benefits representative in the human resources department of a large company. The company is planning a holiday party two months from now. It is your responsibility to produce a poster to invite employees and their families to this annual event. Posters will appear throughout the company, starting next month.

You are about to meet with a representative from your company's graphic arts department. You wish to discuss the best way to advertise the party. Your biggest concerns are time, cost and producing a poster that is attractive as well as informative.

Guidelines

This role play gives the provider an opportunity to use his or her skills to gain an understanding of your needs and expectations. Respond to the provider in a natural way.

In role-playing, do not give the provider all the details of your situation or share all the information you have. Wait for the provider to ask you questions. If the provider asks you a closed question, respond with only a brief 'yes' or 'no'. Do not elaborate unless you are asked an open or high-gain question.

In the final part of the role-play the provider restates his or her understanding of your needs. The provider does not offer you a solution.

Preparation

1. List some of your requirements for, and expectations of, the poster. Here are some ideas you may wish to consider. Add your own if you wish.

   ● Size
   ● Colours
   ● Budget.

2. Consider how important it is to you to execute this poster campaign successfully. Decide on the feelings you wish to convey in this interaction.

Reproduced from *Customer Service Games for Training*, Graham Roberts-Phelps, Gower, Aldershot

2: Graphic arts department provider

Situation

You work in the graphic arts department of a large company. You are about to meet with an internal customer from the human resources department about designing a poster to promote a holiday party the company is giving for its employees and their families.

Guidelines

You consider yourself as a high-quality provider. This role play gives you an opportunity to practise welcoming, listening, asking questions and restating the customer's feelings and facts. Focus on obtaining as much information as possible about the customer's needs, wants and expectations.

In framing your questions, take into consideration what your own needs and interests might be, were you the customer in this situation. What questions might you want to be asked?

In the final part of the role play summarize and restate your understanding of the customer's needs. You are not to offer the customer a solution.

Preparation

1. Make a note of what you will say to open the interaction.
2. What needs and expectations might the customer have? Here are some ideas you may wish to consider. Add your own.

   - Colours
   - Quantity
   - Budget.

3. Formulate questions that will help you discover the customer's needs. Use:

   - Closed questions
   - Open questions
   - High-gain questions.

4. Consider what feelings the customer might have.
5. How might you restate those feelings?
6. See the 'Observation worksheet' to review the skills on which the observer will critique you.

Reproduced from *Customer Service Games for Training*, Graham Roberts-Phelps, Gower, Aldershot

3: Holiday customer

Situation

You have recently had an insurance policy mature. With some of the proceeds you and your family have decided to go on a 'dream' holiday. You decide to visit a local travel agent to discuss options and ideas.

Guidelines

This role play gives the provider an opportunity to use his or her skills to gain an understanding of your needs and expectations. Respond to the provider in a natural way.

In role-playing, do not give the provider all the details of your situation or share all the information you have. Wait for the provider to ask you questions. If the provider asks you a closed question, respond with only a brief 'yes' or 'no'. Do not elaborate unless you are asked an open or high-gain question.

In the final part of the role-play the provider restates his or her understanding of your needs. The provider does not offer you a solution.

Preparation

1. Consider what type and style of holiday you might like. What will impress you and encourage you to use this agent?
2. Make a list of questions that you might wish to ask.

Reproduced from *Customer Service Games for Training*, Graham Roberts-Phelps, Gower, Aldershot

3: Holiday provider

Situation

Your customer has recently had an insurance policy mature. With some of the proceeds they have decided to go on a 'dream' holiday with their family. They are visiting your travel agency to discuss options and ideas.

Guidelines

You consider yourself as a high-quality provider. This role play gives you an opportunity to practise welcoming, listening, asking questions and restating the customer's feelings and facts. Focus on obtaining as much information as possible about the customer's needs, wants and expectations.

In framing your questions, take into consideration what your own needs and interests might be, were you the customer in this situation. What questions might you want to be asked?

In the final part of the role play summarize and restate your understanding of the customer's needs. You are not to offer the customer a solution.

Preparation

1. Make a note of what you will say to open the interaction.
2. What needs and expectations might the customer have? Consider what might be important to them in choosing their holiday. How can you encourage them to book with you?
3. Formulate questions that will help you discover the customer's needs. Use:

   - Closed questions
   - Open questions
   - High-gain questions.

4. Consider what feelings the customer might have.
5. How might you restate those feelings?
6. See the 'Observation worksheet' to review the skills on which the observer will critique you.

Reproduced from *Customer Service Games for Training*, Graham Roberts-Phelps, Gower, Aldershot

4: Apartment rental customer

Situation

You are looking for an apartment to rent. You are open to exploring rentals in different neighbourhoods in your city. You have been referred to CK Rentals, a firm that specializes in apartment listings.

Guidelines

This role play gives the provider an opportunity to use his or her skills to gain an understanding of your needs and expectations. Respond to the provider in a natural way.

In role-playing, do not give the provider all the details of your situation or share all the information you have. Wait for the provider to ask you questions. If the provider asks you a closed question, respond with only a brief 'yes' or 'no'. Do not elaborate unless you are asked an open or high-gain question.

In the final part of the role-play the provider restates his or her understanding of your needs. The provider does not offer you a solution.

Preparation

1. List your requirements for, and expectations of, a desirable apartment. Here are some ideas you may wish to consider. Add your own if you wish.

    ● Two bedrooms
    ● Access to public transport
    ● Reasonable rent.

2. Consider how important finding the right apartment is to you. Decide on the feelings you wish to convey in this interaction.

Reproduced from *Customer Service Games for Training*, Graham Roberts-Phelps, Gower, Aldershot

4: Apartment rental provider

Situation

You are a representative for CK Rentals, a firm that specializes in apartment listings for professional people. CK Rentals, with its extensive listings, enjoys an excellent reputation for finding the 'right' apartments for its customers. You are about to talk to a potential customer who is looking for an apartment.

Guidelines

You consider yourself a high-quality provider. This role play gives you an opportunity to practise welcoming, listening, asking questions and restating the customer's feelings and facts. Focus on obtaining as much information as possible about the customer's needs, wants and expectations.

In framing your questions, take into consideration what your own needs and interests might be, were you the customer in this situation. What questions might you want to be asked?

In the final part of the role play summarize and restate your understanding of the customer's needs. You are not to offer the customer a solution.

Preparation

1. Make a note of what you will say to open the interaction.
2. What needs and expectations might the customer have? Here are some ideas you may wish to consider. Add your own.

   - Rent and utilities costs
   - Neighbourhood
   - Important features

3. Formulate questions that will help you discover the customer's needs. Use:

   - Closed questions
   - Open questions
   - High-gain questions.

4. Consider what feelings the customer might have.
5. How might you restate those feelings?
6. See the 'Observation worksheet' to review the skills on which the observer will critique you.

Reproduced from *Customer Service Games for Training*, Graham Roberts-Phelps, Gower, Aldershot

5: Electronics customer

Situation

You have recently redecorated your home, and you now wish to surprise your family with a home entertainment system. You are particularly interested in sound equipment yourself, and your children would be excited about a new TV set. You are about to talk to a customer representative from a home electronics outlet about what kind of system you might put together.

Guidelines

This role play gives the provider an opportunity to use his or her skills to gain an understanding of your needs and expectations. Respond to the provider in a natural way.

In role-playing, do not give the provider all the details of your situation or share all the information you have. Wait for the provider to ask you questions. If the provider asks you a closed question, respond with only a brief 'yes' or 'no'. Do not elaborate unless you are asked an open or high-gain question.

In the final part of the role play the provider restates his or her understanding of your needs. The provider does not offer you a solution.

Preparation

1. List your requirements for, and expectations of, an entertainment system. Here are some ideas you may wish to consider. Add your own if you wish.

   - TV set with remote control
   - Stereo sound capability
   - Wide-screen TV
   - Budget.

2. Consider how important the home entertainment system is to you. Decide on the feelings you wish to convey in this interaction.

Reproduced from *Customer Service Games for Training*, Graham Roberts-Phelps, Gower, Aldershot

5: Electronics provider

Situation

You are a customer representative for a home electronics outlet. You have been approached by a customer who is interested in a home entertainment system. Adults and children will be using the system which the customer selects.

Guidelines

You consider yourself as a high-quality provider. This role play gives you an opportunity to practise welcoming, listening, asking questions and restating the customer's feelings and facts. Focus on obtaining as much information as possible about the customer's needs, wants and expectations.

In framing your questions, take into consideration what your own needs and interests might be, were you the customer in this situation. What questions might you want to be asked?

In the final part of the role play summarize and restate your understanding of the customer's needs. You are not to offer the customer a solution.

Preparation

1. Make a note of what you will say to open the interaction.
2. What needs and expectations might the customer have? Here are some ideas you may wish to consider. Add your own.

   ● Components
   ● Local service centres
   ● Ease of use.

3. Formulate questions that will help you discover the customer's needs. Use:

   ● Closed questions
   ● Open questions
   ● High-gain questions.

4. Consider what feelings the customer might have.
5. How might you restate those feelings?
6. See the 'Observation worksheet' to review the skills on which the observer will critique you.

Reproduced from *Customer Service Games for Training*, Graham Roberts-Phelps, Gower, Aldershot

6: Restaurant customer

Situation

This morning you learned that several of your office colleagues are planning to get together this evening after work, and you have been selected to host the group at your home. You wish that you had been given advance notice of this event, because you enjoy cooking and would like to prepare a meal for your colleagues. Cooking, of course, is out of the question at this point.

One of the colleagues who will be your guest this evening is celebrating a birthday tomorrow. You would like to do something special for her tonight.

You have decided to call Lorenzo's, part of a local restaurant chain, to order dinner for your guests. You have been pleased with Lorenzo's food and service on several occasions. In fact, you are a loyal customer.

Guidelines

This role play gives the provider an opportunity to use his or her skills to gain an understanding of your needs and expectations. Respond to the provider in a natural way.

In role-playing, do not give the provider all the details of your situation or share all the information you have. Wait for the provider to ask you questions. If the provider asks you a closed question, respond with only a brief 'yes' or 'no'. Do not elaborate unless you are asked an open or high-gain question.

In the final part of the role play the provider restates his or her understanding of your needs. The provider does not offer you a solution.

Preparation

1. List your requirements for, and expectations of, a dinner your guests will enjoy. Here are some ideas you may wish to consider. Add your own if you wish.

   ● Time
   ● Special menu items
   ● Desserts for special occasions.

2. Consider the image of yourself you wish to project to your colleagues. Decide on the feelings you wish to convey in this interaction.

Reproduced from *Customer Service Games for Training*, Graham Roberts-Phelps, Gower, Aldershot

6: Restaurant provider

Situation

You work at Lorenzo's, a family restaurant. Lorenzo's enjoys an excellent reputation for its speed of service, reasonable prices and customer focus. Recently, Lorenzo's has added pizza, international specialities and a variety of desserts to its standard menu of hamburgers, French fries, chicken sandwiches and soft drinks. You are about to talk to a customer who is calling to order dinner.

Guidelines

You consider yourself as a high-quality provider. This role play gives you an opportunity to practise welcoming, listening, asking questions and restating the customer's feelings and facts. Focus on obtaining as much information as possible about the customer's needs, wants and expectations.

In framing your questions, take into consideration what your own needs and interests might be, were you the customer in this situation. What questions might you want to be asked?

In the final part of the role play summarize and restate your understanding of the customer's needs. You are not to offer the customer a solution.

Preparation

1. Make a note of what you will say to open the interaction.
2. What needs and expectations might the customer have? Here are some ideas you may wish to consider. Add your own.

   - Number of people
   - Time
   - Celebrating a special occasion?

3. Formulate questions that will help you discover the customer's needs. Use:

   - Closed questions
   - Open questions
   - High-gain questions.

4. Consider what feelings the customer might have.
5. How might you restate those feelings?
6. See the 'Observation worksheet' to review the skills on which the observer will critique you.

Reproduced from *Customer Service Games for Training*, Graham Roberts-Phelps, Gower, Aldershot

7: Help desk customer

Situation

You have recently been provided with new project management application software to help you manage your projects in a more consistent manner. Before you open it you would like to get a briefing from the Help Desk on the best way to use the new program, as well as tips on how it is linked to other project management applications. You have decided to call the Help Desk for guidance.

Guidelines

This role play gives the provider an opportunity to use his or her skills to gain an understanding of your needs and expectations. Respond to the provider in a natural way.

In role-playing, do not give the provider all the details of your situation or share all the information you have. Wait for the provider to ask you questions. If the provider asks you a closed question, respond with only a brief 'yes' or 'no'. Do not elaborate unless you are asked an open or high-gain question.

In the final part of the role play the provider restates his or her understanding of your needs. The provider does not offer you a solution.

Preparation

1. List some of your requirements for and expectations of specific services. Here are some ideas you may wish to consider. Add your own if you wish.

   - Installation information
   - Opening and tutorials
   - How to use
   - Troubleshooting.

2. Consider how important the problem is to you. Decide on the feelings you wish to convey in this interaction.

7: Help desk provider

Situation

You are a provider working on the Help Desk for your organization. You provide help and guidance to users on hardware as well as software applications. You pride yourself on your ability to answer most user questions, although you do have available technical resources if you run into a difficult problem. You are about to talk to a customer who is calling in about a new software application program.

Guidelines

You consider yourself as a high-quality provider. This role play gives you an opportunity to practise welcoming, listening, asking questions and restating the customer's feelings and facts. Focus on obtaining as much information as possible about the customer's needs, wants and expectations.

In framing your questions, take into consideration what your own needs and interests might be, were you the customer in this situation. What questions might you want to be asked?

In the final part of the role play summarize and restate your understanding of the customer's needs. You are not to offer the customer a solution.

Preparation

1. Make a note of what you will say to open the interaction.
2. What needs and expectations might the customer have? Here are some ideas you may wish to consider. Add your own.

   - Installation information
   - Opening and tutorials
   - How to use
   - Troubleshooting.

3. Formulate questions that will help you discover the customer's needs. Use:

   - Closed questions
   - Open questions
   - High-gain questions.

4. Consider what feelings the customer might have.
5. How might you restate those feelings?
6. See the 'Observation worksheet' to review the skills on which the observer will critique you.

Reproduced from *Customer Service Games for Training*, Graham Roberts-Phelps, Gower, Aldershot

8: Invoiced customer

Situation

You are a customer of your organization, who has recently received an invoice that has raised several concerns. Your first concern has to do with the completion of the work for which you are being billed. You are not clear that it has all been completed satisfactorily. Second, you have questions as to how the amount was calculated. You do not see any listing of hours, rates or materials. Third, you are not clear as to how the amount billed relates to the deliverables on the contract. You have decided to call the business service provider to get some answers.

Guidelines

This role play gives the provider an opportunity to use his or her skills to gain an understanding of your needs and expectations. Respond to the provider in a natural way.

In role-playing, do not give the provider all the details of your situation or share all the information you have. Wait for the provider to ask you questions. If the provider asks you a closed question, respond with only a brief 'yes' or 'no'. Do not elaborate unless you are asked an open or high-gain question.

In the final part of the role play the provider restates his or her understanding of your needs. The provider does not offer you a solution.

Preparation

1. List some of your requirements for, and expectations of, the invoice. Here are some ideas you may wish to consider. Add your own if you wish.

   - Work being billed
   - Hours and rates
   - Contract deliverables.

2. Consider how important it is to you to have a complete and accurate invoice. Decide on the feelings you wish to convey in this interaction.

Reproduced from *Customer Service Games for Training*, Graham Roberts-Phelps, Gower, Aldershot

8: Invoice provider

Situation

You are a service provider handling customer questions and problems in the billing and invoicing area. Your responsibilities include dealing with customer questions on the invoices sent by your line of business to customers. Typical issues include questions on amounts, rates, dates and amount of work accomplished versus the amount billed. You are about to talk with a customer who has called about an invoice that was recently sent.

Guidelines

You consider yourself as a high-quality provider. This role play gives you an opportunity to practise welcoming, listening, asking questions and restating the customer's feelings and facts. Focus on obtaining as much information as possible about the customer's needs, wants and expectations.

In framing your questions, take into consideration what your own needs and interests might be, were you the customer in this situation. What questions might you want to be asked?

In the final part of the role play summarize and restate your understanding of the customer's needs. You are not to offer the customer a solution.

Preparation

1. Make a note of what you will say to open the interaction.
2. What needs and expectations might the customer have? Here are some ideas you may wish to consider. Add your own.

   - Work being billed
   - Hours and rates
   - Contract deliverables.

3. Formulate questions that will help you discover the customer's needs. Use:

   - Closed questions
   - Open questions
   - High-gain questions.

4. Consider what feelings the customer might have.
5. How might you restate those feelings?
6. See the 'Observation worksheet' to review the skills on which the observer will critique you.

Reproduced from *Customer Service Games for Training*, Graham Roberts-Phelps, Gower, Aldershot

9: Contract customer

Situation

You are a customer who has contracted on a time-and-materials basis with an organization for project consulting. You have received the work breakdown structure and project plan, and have several concerns. You feel that the schedule that has been included for the project is over-optimistic, and, in your experience, projects of this magnitude have not been completed on time in the past. Second, you feel that the cost estimates are also low and that you may face overruns as the project is implemented. You would like to receive some assurances that your organization feels this is a realistic price and time frame, since you need to budget the amount and cannot go back for additional funding.

Guidelines

This role play gives the provider an opportunity to use his or her skills to gain an understanding of your needs and expectations. Respond to the provider in a natural way.

In role-playing, do not give the provider all the details of your situation or share all the information you have. Wait for the provider to ask you questions. If the provider asks you a closed question, respond with only a brief 'yes' or 'no'. Do not elaborate unless you are asked an open or high-gain question.

In the final part of the role play the provider restates his or her understanding of your needs. The provider does not offer you a solution.

Preparation

1. List some of your requirements for the work breakdown structure and project plan. Consider the information that the provider will probably request and be prepared to give details. Here are some ideas you may wish to consider. Add your own if you wish.

   ● How was the estimated cost determined?
   ● How realistic is the schedule?
   ● How confident can you be that there will be no overruns in terms of cost or schedule?

2. Consider how important the work breakdown structure and project plan is to you. Decide on the feelings you wish to convey in this interaction.

Reproduced from *Customer Service Games for Training*, Graham Roberts-Phelps, Gower, Aldershot

9: Contract provider

Situation

You are a service provider responsible for handling contractual issues in the area of pricing and scheduling. Many of your customers enquire about the basis of contract pricing, as well as about issues of cost overruns, organizational responsibility for project costs and the like. While you try to answer all their questions, sometimes you need to contact project leaders for answers to complex problems. You are about to talk with a customer with some concerns about a time-and-materials contract.

Guidelines

You consider yourself as a high-quality provider. This role play gives you an opportunity to practise welcoming, listening, asking questions and restating the customer's feelings and facts. Focus on obtaining as much information as possible about the customer's needs, wants and expectations.

In framing your questions, take into consideration what your own needs and interests might be, were you the customer in this situation. What questions might you want to be asked?

In the final part of the role play summarize and restate your understanding of the customer's needs. You are not to offer the customer a solution.

Preparation

1. Make a note of what you will say to open the interaction.
2. What needs and expectations might the customer have? Here are some ideas you may wish to consider. Add your own.

   - How was the estimated cost determined?
   - How realistic is the schedule?
   - How confident can you be that there will be no overruns in cost or schedule?

3. Formulate questions that will help you discover the customer's needs. Use:

   - Closed questions
   - Open questions
   - High-gain questions.

4. Consider what feelings the customer might have.
5. How might you restate those feelings?
6. See the 'Observation worksheet' to review the skills on which the observer will critique you.

Reproduced from *Customer Service Games for Training*, Graham Roberts-Phelps, Gower, Aldershot

10: Documentation customer

Situation

You are working on a project involving considerable system documentation. Your project requires equipment and operation documentation from vendors and suppliers, as well as new documentation being generated by your organization's consultants and technicians. The project is well underway, and you have several concerns. First, you have not received any documentation from the software and hardware vendors who are suppliers to your organization. You would like to know more about the availability and format of this material. Second, you would like to know how your organization plans to integrate all the documentation, standard and new, into a seamless user-friendly, easily accessed format. Third, you would like to know more about the schedule for completion of all documentation.

Guidelines

This role play gives the provider an opportunity to use his or her skills to gain an understanding of your needs and expectations. Respond to the provider in a natural way.

In role-playing, do not give the provider all the details of your situation or share all the information you have. Wait for the provider to ask you questions. If the provider asks you a closed question, respond with only a brief 'yes' or 'no'. Do not elaborate unless you are asked an open or high-gain question.

In the final part of the role play the provider restates his or her understanding of your needs. The provider does not offer you a solution.

Preparation

1. List your requirements for and expectations of system documentation. Here are some ideas you may wish to consider. Add your own if you wish.

    - Availability of documentation
    - Format of documentation
    - User interface.

2. Consider how important integrated system documentation is to you. Decide on the feelings you wish to convey in this interaction.

Reproduced from *Customer Service Games for Training*, Graham Roberts-Phelps, Gower, Aldershot

10: Documentation service provider

Situation

You are a service provider in your organization, with responsibilities for dealing with documentation and technical publications issues. You help customers with issues around the scheduling, formatting, pricing and integration of project documentation. You serve as a liaison between the customer and those actually creating the documentation. You are about to talk with a customer who is working on a project that is well underway, but who has concerns about system documentation.

Guidelines

You consider yourself as a high-quality provider. This role play gives you an opportunity to practise welcoming, listening, asking questions and restating the customer's feelings and facts. Focus on obtaining as much information as possible about the customer's needs, wants and expectations.

In framing your questions, take into consideration what your own needs and interests might be, were you the customer in this situation. What questions might you want to be asked?

In the final part of the role play, summarize and restate your understanding of the customer's needs. You are not to offer the customer a solution.

Preparation

1. Make a note of what you will say to open the interaction.
2. What needs and expectations might the customer have? Here are some ideas you may wish to consider. Add your own.

    ● Availability of documentation
    ● Format of documentation
    ● User interface.

3. Formulate questions that will help you discover the customer's needs. Use:

    ● Closed questions
    ● Open questions
    ● High-gain questions.

4. What feelings might the customer have?
5. How might you restate those feelings?
6. See the 'Observation worksheet' to review the skills on which the observer will critique you.

Reproduced from *Customer Service Games for Training*, Graham Roberts-Phelps, Gower, Aldershot

Flip Chart Games for Trainers

Graham Roberts-Phelps

For many trainers, the flip chart is - and always will be - the simplest and most flexible instant training aid. For any line manager or team leader, working in their new role as trainer and developer, the flip chart may be the only training aid available to them. Hence this collection of *Flip Chart Games for Trainers*.

The 50 exercises, activities and games all revolve around or make active use of a flip chart. In some cases the trainer facilitates the session using the flip chart; in others, it's the participants who use it as part of the exercise. However, whether it's a short icebreaker such as *Jargon Jumble* or *Reasons to Learn*, an energizer such as *Team Talents* or a summarizing exercise such as *Cartoon Time*, or *Jigsaw*, the *Flip Chart Games for Trainers* is certain to engage the imagination and the visual sense of your participants.

Many of the games and exercises can be run in as little as 15 to 25 minutes, making them equally suitable for short meetings or extended training courses. The 'Variations' section helps you to create multiple applications for the exercises, or, if you wish, develop them into a longer training activity.

The flip chart is the essential tool for trainers and facilitators and *Flip Chart Games for Trainers* is likely to become as necessary a training aid as the flip charts themselves. A great collection for anyone wishing to inject fun, increase learning and encourage involvement in any session that they run.

Gower

Games for Trainers

3 Volume Set

Andy Kirby

Most trainers use games. And trainers who use games collect new games. Andy Kirby's three-volume compendium contain 75 games in each volume. They range from icebreakers and energizers to substantial exercises in communication. Each game is presented in a standard format which includes summary, statement of objectives, list of materials required, recommended timings and step-by-step instructions for running the event. Photocopiable masters are provided for any materials needed by participants.

All the games are indexed by objectives, and Volume 1 contains an introduction analysing the different kinds of game, setting out the benefits they offer and explaining how to use games to the maximum advantage. It is a programmed text designed to help trainers to develop their own games. Volume 3 reflects current trends in training; in particular the increased attention being paid to stress management and assertiveness. Volumes 2 and 3 contain an integrated index covering all three volumes.

Gower

Gower Handbook of Training and Development

Third Edition

Edited by Anthony Landale

It is now crystal clear that, in today's ever-changing world, an organization's very survival depends upon how it supports its people to learn and keep on learning. Of course this new imperative has considerable implications for trainers who are now playing an increasingly critical role in supporting individuals, teams and business management. In this respect today's trainers may need to be more than excellent presenters; they are also likely to require a range of consultancy and coaching skills, to understand the place of technology in supporting learning and be able to align personal development values with business objectives.

This new edition of the *Gower Handbook of Training and Development* will be an invaluable aid for today's training professional as they face up to the organizational challenges presented to them. All 38 chapters in this edition are new and many of the contributors, whilst being best-selling authors or established industry figures, are appearing for the first time in this form. Edited by Anthony Landale, this *Handbook* builds on the foundations that previous editions have laid down whilst, at the same time, highlighting many of the very latest advances in the industry.

The *Handbook* is divided into five sections - learning organization, best practice, advanced techniques in training and development, the use of IT in learning, and evaluation issues.

Gower

Outdoor Games for Trainers

Carmine Consalvo

Games are perennially popular as a training method for developing teamworking and problem-solving skills. Consalvo has collected together 63 games specifically designed for outdoor use. All of the events can be conducted easily and safely with the minimum of materials and preparation. Many of them can be run equally well indoors.

Each activity is presented in a standard format that includes a summary, a statement of objectives, a note of any materials required, approximate timings and detailed guidance on what to do, when and how, covering both content and process. The exercises vary in length from a few minutes to over an hour. Titles reflect their inventiveness, ranging from: *Space Escape* to *Shuffling the Deck*, and from *Wet Dog Wiggle* to *Ostrich Eggs*. Together they provide a rich store of adventure, energy and memorable learning.

Gower

Sales Training Games

For Sales Managers and Trainers

Graham Roberts-Phelps

Selling is a skill that should not be limited to sales staff. Customer service, or other support staff, could all benefit from developing an awareness of and an ability to sell to customers. Also, the opportunity for developing those skills should not be limited to sales training workshops.

Here, at last, is a mix of over 80 games, exercises and ideas that can be used to develop sales, customer service and other staff. They range from simple 'skill boosters' for coaching sessions or team meetings, through icebreakers, energizers and selling quizzes to full blown role plays and case studies.

The principle at the heart of all the material is that games and exercises should be generic - transferable across different organizations and sales situations - and that they should use an 'open content' approach. This means that participants must supply their own examples and experiences, to make the material immediately and completely relevant.

This collection of games and exercises will enable sales managers or trainers to:

• develop their people with confidence, secure in the knowledge that all of the material has been thoroughly road-tested on courses and seminars;
• ensure a flexible approach, varying their pace or style in response to the subject matter and their audience;
• reinforce the learning, using different formats of exercise to cover the same learning points;
• train (rather than talk), using the material to encourage people to start using what they already know.

Gower

Team Development Games for Trainers

Roderick R Stuart

If you're involved in designing or delivering interpersonal skills training you will know that there are two perennial problems. The first is finding material that matches your objectives. The second is finding material that will be unfamiliar to the participants.

The 59 games in Roderick Stuart's collection have not appeared in print before. Based on the author's experience with a wide range of organizations and participants, they cover the entire gamut of skills associated with team development, including assertiveness, communication, creativity, decision making, influencing, listening, planning, problem solving and time management.

Each game is presented in a standard format, with an indication of objectives, timing and group size, detailed step-by-step guidance for the trainer or team leader, and ready-to-copy masters for all participants' material. An index of objectives makes it easy to select the most suitable items for your training needs and to compile complete workshops or more extensive programmes. In addition the author provides a four-stage model that relates learning to the requirements of the workplace, and a set of checklists for facilitating the learning process.

Gower